Inspirational Proverbs and Sayings

Rebecca Milner

Level 3
(1600-word)

IBC パブリッシング

はじめに

　ラダーシリーズは、「はしご (ladder)」を使って一歩一歩上を目指すように、学習者の実力に合わせ、無理なくステップアップできるよう開発された英文リーダーのシリーズです。

　リーディング力をつけるためには、繰り返したくさん読むこと、いわゆる「多読」がもっとも効果的な学習法であると言われています。多読では、「1. 速く 2. 訳さず英語のまま 3. なるべく辞書を使わず」に読むことが大切です。スピードを計るなど、速く読むよう心がけましょう（たとえば TOEIC® テストの音声スピードはおよそ 1 分間に 150 語です）。そして 1 語ずつ訳すのではなく、英語を英語のまま理解するくせをつけるようにします。こうして読み続けるうちに語感がついてきて、だんだんと英語が理解できるようになるのです。まずは、ラダーシリーズの中からあなたのレベルに合った本を選び、少しずつ英文に慣れ親しんでください。たくさんの本を手にとるうちに、英文書がすらすら読めるようになってくるはずです。

《本シリーズの特徴》
- 中学校レベルから中級者レベルまで5段階に分かれています。自分に合ったレベルからスタートしてください。
- クラシックから現代文学、ノンフィクション、ビジネスと幅広いジャンルを扱っています。あなたの興味に合わせてタイトルを選べます。
- 巻末のワードリストで、いつでもどこでも単語の意味を確認できます。レベル1、2では、文中の全ての単語が、レベル3以上は中学校レベル外の単語が掲載されています。
- カバーにヘッドホーンマークのついているタイトルは、オーディオ・サポートがあります。ウェブから購入／ダウンロードし、リスニング教材としても併用できます。

《使用語彙について》

レベル1：中学校で学習する単語約1000語

レベル2：レベル1の単語＋使用頻度の高い単語約300語

レベル3：レベル1の単語＋使用頻度の高い単語約600語

レベル4：レベル1の単語＋使用頻度の高い単語約1000語

レベル5：語彙制限なし

Contents

Success 1

Love & Friendships 27

Human Nature 47

Good Advice 61

Lessons for Living 81

Word List 108

読みはじめる前に

本書では、人間の生き方、人生の真実について、言いやすく、簡潔にまとめた言葉を100集めました。庶民の生活や知恵から出た教訓や戒めのほか、ビジネスマン、映画監督、野球選手などの心に残る言葉もあります。

格言の著者 (頭の数字は、該当する格言の番号です。)

1

Ralph Waldo Emerson (1803-1882) ラルフ・ワルド・エマーソン
ハーバード大学を卒業後は神学校で学び、牧師の資格をとる。代表作に「自然論」「偉人論」など。「あなた以外にあなたに平和をもたらすものはいない」などの言葉がある。

3, 20, 92

Ben Franklin (1706-1790) ベンジャミン・フランクリン
アメリカ独立に、政治家として貢献した。ビジネスマンとして成功した後、自然科学の発明にも貢献。現在の100ドル紙幣に肖像が描かれている。「信用は金なり」とも言っている。

6

Yogi Berra (1925-) ヨギ・ベラ
メジャーリーグのヤンキースで活躍したプロ野球選手。背番号8は永久欠番になっている。ユーモアあふれる発言で、今でもアメリカ人に親しまれている。

9

Joseph P. Kennedy (1888-1969) ジョセフ・P・ケネディ
合衆国史上最も若く、かつ初のカトリック教徒として大統領となったJ・F・ケネディの父として知られるが、本人も民主党の大物政治家だった。金融業、映画会社、スコッチの輸入などで財を成した。

12

Frank Leahy (1908-1973) フランク・リーヒー
アメリカン・フットボールの選手。ボストン大学、ノートルダム大学でコーチとして活躍。

13

Herman Edwards (1954-) ハーマン・エドワーズ
フィラデルフィアのアメリカン・フットボールチーム、イーグルスで10年間、コーナーバックとして活躍。ニューヨーク・ジェッツのヘッドコーチも務める。

15

Thomas Edison (1847-1931) トーマス・エジソン

生涯の発明は1300にのぼるといわれるアメリカの発明王。電話機、蓄音機などの発明は誰もが知っているところ。GE社の設立者としても有名。

17

Andrew Carnegie *(1835-1919)* アンドリュー・カーネギー
実業家、大富豪。12歳で紡績工場で働き始め、以来現場から努力しビジネスを学ぶ。後に鉄鋼王と呼ばれる。「チャンスに出会わない人はいない。それをものにできるかどうかだ」など。

22

Walt Disney *(1901-1966)* ウォルト・ディズニー
誰もが知る「ミッキーマウス」や「ディズニーランド」の生みの親。一族はアイルランドからの移民。幼少期から絵を描くのが好きで、一生夢を追い続けた。他の言葉に、「不可能なことは何もない」

25

Daniel Webster *(1782-1852)* ダニエル・ウェブスター
アメリカの政治家、法律家。貧しい農家の生まれだが、教育熱心だった両親のおかげで、ダートマス大学を卒業、弁護士としても活躍。

29, 33

Eleanor Roosevelt *(1884-1962)* エレノア・ルーズベルト
アメリカ第32代大統領フランクリン・ルーズベルトのファーストレディーとしてよく知られている。国連のアメリカ代表も務め、数々の名言を残している。

36, 54

Abraham Lincoln *(1809-1865)* エイブラハム・リンカーン
アメリカ国民に最も愛された大統領の一人。ケンタッキー州の貧しい農家で生まれ、独学で法律を学んだ。「奴隷解放の父」とも称される。

41

Jimi Hendrix *(1942-1970)* ジミ・ヘンドリックス
日本では「ジミヘン」と呼ばれて愛された、アメリカのミュージシャン。黒人の父、インディアンの母との間にシアトルで生まれる。天才的なギターテクニックで、ミュージシャンに大きな影響を与えた。

45

Billy Wilder *(1906-2002)* ビリー・ワイルダー
オーストリア出身の新聞記者、脚本家。ユダヤ人であったため、ナチの台頭とともにメキシコを経てアメリカに移民。「お熱いのがお好き」「アパートの鍵貸します」などの脚本で有名。

48

Leo Durocher *(1906-1991)* レオ・ドローチャー
マサチューセッツ州生まれの野球選手。ヤンキース、ドジャースの選手

として活躍した後、監督になり、通算2008勝を記録している。

51
Dr. Seuss *(1904-1991)* ドクター・スース
マサチューセッツ州生まれの絵本作家。現代のマザー・グースとも言われる、代表作「The Cat in the Hat」は、世界中の子供に愛されている。

56
Muhammad Ali *(1942-)* モハメド・アリ
ケンタッキー州生まれのボクシングの元世界チャンピオン。本名、カシアス・クレイ。1960年のオリンピックで金メダルをとったが、当時のアメリカ社会は、まだ黒人差別が激しく、祝賀ムードもなかったという。怒った彼は、金メダルを川に投げ捨てたという逸話もある。

69
Bert Lance *(1931-)* バート・ランス
アメリカの実業家であり、カーター政権の行政管理予算局長。「壊れていないものを修理するな」は、1977年の雑誌「Nation's Business」に掲載された言葉。

76
Abbie Hoffman *(1936-1989)* アビー・ホフマン
ユダヤ人家庭に生まれ、マサチューセッツ州で育つ。政治活動家。1968年にはベトナム反戦を訴え、逮捕された経歴を持つ。

78
Mark Twain *(1835-1910)* マーク・トウェイン
「トム・ソーヤーの冒険」などで知られるアメリカの作家。数多くの小説、エッセーを世に送り出した。「これまで思い悩んだことのうち、98パーセントは取り越し苦労だった」なども彼の言葉。

81
Stephen King *(1947-)* スティーヴン・キング
「モダン・ホラーの旗手」とも呼ばれるアメリカの人気作家。彼の作品は次々とベストセラーになり、世界中で翻訳、また映画化されている。

83
Andy Warhol *(1928-1987)* アンディ・ウォーホル
アメリカの画家、芸術家。両親はチェコスロバキアからの移民。キャンベル・スープの缶をモチーフにするなど、ポップアートの生みの親として知られる。

85
Ann Landers *(1918-2002)* アン・ランダース
専業主婦・母だったイッピー・レダラー（本名）は、シカゴ・サンタイムズの「Ask Ann Landers」というコラムを任されることになる。以来、

アン・ランダースとして読者からの数々の質問に答え続けた名物コラムニスト。

87
Albert Einstein (1879-1955) アルベルト・アインシュタイン
ドイツ生まれのユダヤ人。相対性理論、ブラウン運動など数々の業績を残した物理学者。偉大な学者にも関わらず、「自分は天才ではなく、ただ一つのことをやり続けただけだ」と言っている。

89
Woody Allen (1935-) ウディ・アレン
大学時代から新聞、雑誌にジョークなどを投稿していたというユーモアセンスあふれる映画監督、俳優。アカデミー監督賞、脚本賞を受賞するも、式には出ないなどハリウッドには背を向けた人としても有名。

90
Harley L. Lutz (1882-1975) ハーレー・L・ルッツ
国家財政、税金についての研究に生涯をかけた経済学者。政府の歳出が増加することに対して、厳しく批判した。

93
Jack Welch (1935-) ジャック・ウェルチ
1981年から20年間、ゼネラル・エレクトリックのCEOを務めたアメリカの実業家。「フォーチュン」誌で、20世紀最高の経営者にも選ばれたことがある。

94
Bob Dylan (1941-) ボブ・ディラン
アメリカ公民権賛同歌として知られる「風に吹かれて」の作者、ミュージシャン。メッセージ性の強い楽曲を数多く残し、アメリカ音楽界にも多大な影響を与えてきた。

96
Franklin D. Roosevelt (1882-1945) フランクリン・デラノ・ルーズベルト
ニューヨークの裕福な地主の家に生まれる。第32代アメリカ大統領。史上唯一、4選を果たした大統領として知られる。経済立て直しのためニューディール政策を推進したことで知られる。

97
Booker T. Washington (1856-1915) ブッカー・T・ワシントン
奴隷として生まれた彼は、南北戦争後にようやく自由を得、学校に通うようになる。後に有名な教育者となり、黒人のための高等教育機関を設立した。黒人として、アメリカ史上初めて、切手のモデルに採用された。

98
Liza Minnelli (1946-) ライザ・ミネリ

わずか2歳で映画デビューしたというアメリカの女優で歌手。アルコール依存症、難病などを克服し、その度に第一線にカムバックした。ブロードウェイミュージカル、映画など多数の作品に出演。

99
L. Frank Baum (1856–1919) ライマン・フランク・ボーム
「オズの魔法使い」で知られるアメリカの児童文学作家。裕福な家庭に育つが、父の死後は経済的困難に陥り、オズシリーズが成功するまでは苦労する。60編以上の童話や文学作品を執筆した。

格言の意味

1 Nothing great was ever achieved without enthusiasm
情熱なくして偉業が達成されたことはない (p.2)

2 Where there's a will, there's a way
意志ある所に道あり (p.3)

3 Time is money
時は金なり (p.4)

4 Fight fire with fire
目には目を (p.5)

5 Talk is cheap
言うは易し (p.6)

6 It ain't over 'til it's over
勝敗は最後までわからない (p.7)

7 Rome wasn't built in a day
ローマは一日にしてならず (p.8)

8 Opportunity never knocks twice
チャンスは二度やってこない (p.9)

9 Don't get mad, get even
怒るな、やり返せ (p.10)

10 You can't argue with success
論より証拠 (p.11)

11 What goes up must come down
上がるものは必ず下がる (p.12)

12 When the going gets tough, the tough get going

状況が厳しいときはタフな人が成功する *(p.13)*

13 You play to win the game
勝つために戦え *(p.14)*

14 If you can't beat 'em, join 'em
長い物には巻かれろ *(p.15)*

15 There is no substitute for hard work
勤勉に代わるものはない *(p.16)*

16 The early bird catches the worm
早起きは三文の徳 *(p.17)*

17 Success is getting what you want; happiness is wanting what you get
成功は欲しいものを手に入れること、幸福は手に入るものを欲しがること *(p.18)*

18 The squeaky wheel gets the grease
主張すれば見返りを得られる *(p.19)*

19 Actions speak louder than words
口先よりも実践が大事 *(p.20)*

20 There are no gains without pains (No pain, no gain)
苦労なくして得るものなし *(p.21)*

21 If a thing is worth doing, it's worth doing well
やるからには最善を尽くせ *(p.22)*

22 If you can dream it, you can do it
夢見ることができれば、それは実現できる *(p.23)*

23 Two heads are better than one
三人寄れば文殊の知恵 *(p.24)*

24 Strike while the iron is hot
鉄は熱いうちに打て *(p.25)*

25 There's always room at the top
最上の地位はいつでも空いている *(p.26)*

26 Don't judge a book by its cover
見掛けで判断してはいけない *(p.28)*

27 Never mix business with pleasure

遊びと仕事を混同するな *(p.29)*

28 There are plenty of fish in the sea
（恋人にふられても）いい人は、まだたくさんいる *(p.30)*

29 Understanding is a two-way street
理解とは双方向なものだ *(p.31)*

30 It takes two to tango
タンゴは1人では踊れない（責任は両方にある） *(p.32)*

31 Love is blind
恋は盲目 *(p.33)*

32 Time heals all wounds
時はすべての傷をいやす *(p.34)*

33 It is not fair to ask of others what you are unwilling to do yourself
あなたがやりたくないことを他人に頼むのは、フェアではありません *(p.35)*

34 Treat others the way you would like to be treated
自分にしてもらいたいことを人にしてあげなさい *(p.36)*

35 Let sleeping dogs lie
寝た子を起こすな *(p.37)*

36 If you look for the bad in people, you'll surely find it
もし人々の中に「悪」を探すなら、それは確実に見つかるだろう *(p.38)*

37 Absence makes the heart grow fonder
遠ざかるほど想いは募る *(p.39)*

38 If you can't say anything nice, don't say anything at all
もし良いことが言えないのであれば、何も言うな *(p.40)*

39 Two's company, three's a crowd
二人は仲間、三人は人込み *(p.41)*

40 Misery loves company
不幸は道連れを欲しがる *(p.42)*

41 Knowledge speaks, but wisdom listens
知識はものを言う。だが知恵は耳を傾ける *(p.43)*

42 Good fences make good neighbors
親しき仲にも礼儀あり *(p.44)*

43 Good friends are hard to find
いい友達は見つけるのが難しい *(p.45)*

44 The grass is always greener on the other side of the fence
隣の庭の芝生はいつも青い *(p.48)*

45 Hindsight is always 20-20
後悔先に立たず *(p.49)*

46 Nobody is perfect
完璧な人間などいない *(p.50)*

47 Old habits die hard
身についた習慣はなかなか取れない *(p.51)*

48 Nice guys finish last
お人よしでは勝てない *(p.52)*

49 Beauty is only skin deep
美人も皮一重 *(p.53)*

50 Man cannot live on bread alone
人はパンだけで生きるものではない *(p.54)*

51 A person's a person no matter how small
どんなに小さくても人は人 *(p.55)*

52 The apple doesn't fall far from the tree
リンゴは木からあまり遠いところへは落ちない *(p.56)*

53 Hunger is the best sauce
空腹は最上のソース *(p.57)*

54 Most people are about as happy as they make their minds up to be
多くの人は自分が幸福になろうと決心した程度だけ幸福である *(p.58)*

55 One man's trash is another man's treasure
捨てる神あれば拾う神あり *(p.59)*

56 You are as old as you think you are
自分の信じた年齢が、自分の年齢となる *(p.60)*

57 Don't count your chickens before they've hatched
卵がかえる前にニワトリの数を数えても意味がない *(p.62)*

58 If you don't like the heat, get out of the kitchen
仕事の苦しさに耐えられないなら、仕事を変えよ *(p.63)*

59 Don't bite off more than you can chew
自分の能力以上のことをやろうとするな *(p.64)*

60 Money doesn't grow on trees
金のなる木はない *(p.65)*

61 Quit while you're ahead
勝っているうちにやめておけ *(p.66)*

62 Don't bite the hand that feeds you
恩をあだで返すようなことはするな *(p.67)*

63 People in glass houses shouldn't throw stones
ガラスの家に住む者は石を投げてはならない *(p.68)*

64 Don't burn your bridges behind you
渡った橋を燃やしてしまうな *(p.69)*

65 All that glitters is not gold
光るもの全てが金ではない *(p.70)*

66 Be careful what you wish for
願い事をする時は気をつけなさい *(p.71)*

67 What goes around, comes around
自分の行いは自分に返ってくる *(p.72)*

68 The devil is in the details
悪魔は細部に宿る *(p.73)*

69 If it ain't broke, don't fix it
壊れていないものを修理するな *(p.74)*

70 Never say never
絶対にない、ということはない *(p.75)*

71 Where there is smoke, there is fire
火のない所に煙は立たぬ *(p.76)*

72 Don't put all your eggs in one basket
一つのことにすべてを賭けるな *(p.77)*

73 Better safe than sorry

後悔先に立たず *(p.78)*

74 What you don't know can't hurt you
知らぬが仏 *(p.79)*

75 If life hands you a lemon, make lemonade
人生がレモンをくれるならそれでレモネードを作ればいい
（つらい状況でも、ベストを尽くせ） *(p.82)*

76 Today is the first day of the rest of your life
今日は残りの人生最初の日である *(p.83)*

77 Don't sweat the small stuff
小さいことにくよくよするな *(p.84)*

78 Truth is stranger than fiction
事実は小説よりも奇なり *(p.85)*

79 Practice what you preach
人に説くことを自分でも実行しなさい *(p.86)*

80 Every cloud has a silver lining
どんな悪い状況でもどこかに希望があるものだ *(p.87)*

81 Either get busy living or get busy dying
精力的に生きるか、さもなくば慌ただしく死んでいくか *(p.88)*

82 Beggars can't be choosers
乞食はえり好みできない *(p.89)*

83 In the future everyone will be world-famous for fifteen minutes
近い未来に、誰もが世界中で15分間有名になるだろう *(p.90)*

84 You can't have your cake and eat it, too
ケーキは食べたらなくなる *(p.91)*

85 Wake up and smell the coffee
ちゃんと目を覚まして現実を見なさい *(p.92)*

86 Better late than never
遅れても何もしないよりはまし *(p.93)*

87 Anyone who has never made a mistake has never tried anything new
間違いを犯したことのない人は、新しいことに挑戦したことがない人だ *(p.94)*

88 What doesn't kill you only makes you stronger
生きてさえいればどんな経験でも自分自身を強くする *(p.95)*

89 Showing up is 80 percent of life
顔見せは人生の80パーセント *(p.96)*

90 There is no free lunch
ただより高いものはない *(p.97)*

91 It doesn't rain but it pours
降れば土砂降り *(p.98)*

92 A penny saved is a penny earned
ちりも積もれば山となる *(p.99)*

93 Control your own destiny, or someone else will
自らの運命をコントロールせよ。さもなくば、他の誰かがそうするだろう *(p.100)*

94 You don't need a weatherman to tell which way the wind blows
風がどの方向に吹いているのか知るために、天気予報士は必要ない *(p.101)*

95 When in Rome, do as the Romans do
郷に入っては郷に従え *(p.102)*

96 The only thing we have to fear is fear itself
私たちが恐れなければならない唯一のことは、恐れそのものである *(p.103)*

97 Do a common thing in an uncommon way
普通ではない方法で普通のことをするのはすばらしいこと *(p.104)*

98 Reality is something you rise above
現実とは踏み越えていくもの *(p.105)*

99 There's no place like home
わが家にまさるところなし *(p.106)*

100 The best things in life are free
人生で最高のものは、いくらお金を出しても手に入らない *(p.107)*

Success

1

Nothing great was ever achieved without enthusiasm

— *Ralph Waldo Emerson, author (1803–1882)*

Knowledge and skills can take you far in life, but they won't take you all the way. Enthusiasm takes you that extra step. Enthusiasm makes you excited about your work and your life. It makes you happy to get out of bed every morning.

Enthusiasm is the passion that we bring to our work. It is the difference between a good work of art and a great one. It is the difference between a good presentation and a great one. This is because enthusiasm has the power to inspire other people.

Knowledge and skills can be learned, but enthusiasm must come from inside. It comes naturally to a lucky few; others must look deep inside to discover it. Fortunately, enthusiasm spreads. Spend time with people who have passion, and their enthusiasm might spread to you.

2

Where there's a will, there's a way

— proverb

Some goals may seem impossible. However, if you are very determined, you can find a way to succeed.

Imagine you are standing at the edge of a forest. In front of you are thick trees. You can't see beyond the trees; however, you know that what you want is on the other side of the forest. The only problem is that there's no path. How are you going to get through? Will you give up and turn away? Or will you make your own path through the forest, even though you might get lost or hurt along the way?

If you are truly determined, you will make your own path. You will get to the other side no matter what; that is the power of determination.

3

Time is money

— Ben Franklin, author (1706–1790)

The number of hours in a day is limited to just twenty-four. If you waste time, you will be able to do less in those hours. The less you do, the less money you and your business can make. Move quickly and make decisions quickly to make the most of this time.

Ben Franklin said this over two hundred years ago; however, his words are even truer today. We move faster than before thanks to modern technology. We prefer airplanes to buses and emails to telephone calls. Buses are cheaper, but airplanes get us places faster. Telephone calls build good relationships, but emails take less time. With the time you save, you can work more—not that this is always a good thing!

A The next train doesn't leave for thirty minutes. Should we go for a cup of coffee?

B I don't want to wait for the train. Let's take a taxi.

A But taxis are expensive.

B Those extra thirty minutes are more important to me. Remember, *time is money*! Come on, let's go.

4

Fight fire with fire

— *proverb*

Fight back with equal strength. Fight back with equal determination and skill. Many battles are not easily won. Some battles can become ugly, especially if the prize is worth a lot. The greater the value of the prize, the more difficult the battle for it will be. If you hope to win, you had better fight with everything you have.

A Did you see Jim talking to Lisa this morning?

B Yeah, he must have been saying something funny because she was laughing. I can't compete with a guy like Jim.

A Sure you can. But you can't expect Lisa to notice you if you don't even talk to her. Come on, *fight fire with fire*. I bet you can make her laugh, too, if you try.

Talk is cheap

— proverb

Talking about something is easy. Talking doesn't cost anything. Doing something takes more effort. It can take time and money, too.

Just because someone says something that doesn't mean he or she will actually do it. "Saying and doing are two different things" is another proverb that expresses this idea. There is also: "Easier said than done." Since there are several sayings that express this idea, it is clearly an important one to Americans!

Surely you can think of at least one person you know who often says things that he or she doesn't actually do. Maybe this person is you! Give him or her a little reminder that "saying and doing are two different things." "Talk is cheap" is a little more direct and is used between close friends.

A I'm tired of listening to my boss. Someday I'm going to own my own company so I don't have to listen to anyone.

B You are always saying things like that. *Talk is cheap.* You need to actually do something or you'll be in that job forever.

6

It ain't over 'til it's over

— *Yogi Berra, baseball player & manager (1925–)*

Picture this: the score is 7 to 4 and the baseball game is almost over. The losing team doesn't have a chance, right? Now it is time for the last batter. The bases are loaded. He hits the ball out of the park. It's a grand slam and the game finishes 7 to 8.

A lot can happen between "almost over" and "over." It is important to keep trying until the very end. Anything is possible!

- **A** Look at the score. I don't have a chance. I should just go home.
- **B** Hey, don't give up! After all, *it ain't over 'til it's over.*

7

Rome wasn't built in a day

— *proverb*

Great things take time to create. Great things also take hard work. Rome was one of the greatest cities in Western history. However, it took hundreds of years and hundreds of small steps to become great. Great books take years to write; a successful career can take decades to create.

There will also be challenges along the way. It is important to stay positive, be patient, and keep your eyes on the goal.

A How is your business doing?

B It's doing okay. I just don't seem to be making much progress. I thought I'd have a big office by now. I thought I'd have people working for me.

A You will, someday. Those things just take time. Remember that *Rome wasn't built in a day*.

B That's what everyone keeps telling me.

8

Opportunity never knocks twice

— *proverb*

When an opportunity comes, take it. Another one might not come for a long time. Another one might never come.

It is lucky when opportunity knocks on your door. Unfortunately, opportunity sometimes comes at the wrong time. Often, it comes before you are ready for it. When this happens, it is easy to think, "I will wait for a better time." However, a better time might not come. This might be your only chance, so don't miss it. Next time, opportunity might knock on your friend's door or your neighbor's door instead.

A I got offered a new job.

B Hey, that's great!

A Yeah, the position is great. The pay is great. The only problem is that I would have to move to London. I just moved into a new apartment here. I don't want to move again…

B Hey, *opportunity doesn't knock twice*! You should take the job.

≈ 9 ≈
Don't get mad, get even

— *Joseph P. Kennedy, businessman and politician*
(1888–1969)

Joseph P. Kennedy was the father of John F. Kennedy, the 35th president of the United States. He was also a very successful businessman, so he certainly knew about getting ahead! Kennedy may not have been the first person to say, "Don't get mad, get even," but he made the saying famous.

To get even means to get revenge. It is not very kind advice, but there is some truth to it. Anger is a waste of energy; it won't take you anywhere. Instead, turn your anger into action. Action is a lot more likely to help you get ahead. When under control, anger can actually be excellent motivation. The secret is to keep it under control and to use it for good.

∞10∞

You can't argue with success

— *proverb*

Success often doesn't make sense. It can be hard to understand why some products sell millions while others don't. It can be even harder to understand why some people are successful while others aren't. A product can be useless but still a success. A person can be very nice but not a success at all. Unfortunately, in the world of business, it is the success part that matters the most. Even if you don't like someone or something, if it is successful then it is hard to argue against it.

A I can't believe you did that. Don't you think that was a little, uh, unkind.

B It worked, didn't it? And *you can't argue with success*, right?

ೞ 11 ೞ

What goes up must come down

— *proverb*

If you throw a ball into the air, it will fall back down. This is the law of nature. An airplane can't stay in the sky forever.

Someone who rises will also probably fall. It is unusual for a person to stay successful for a long time. Think of an actress who was very popular ten years ago. Is she still as popular now? Probably she isn't. Somebody new will have taken her place at the top.

It's not just people, though. Companies or even countries that are powerful today weren't always so powerful. Some that aren't powerful now used to be very powerful. Getting to the top doesn't mean that you get to stay at the top forever. Everything and everyone come down eventually.

12

When the going gets tough, the tough get going

— *Frank Leahy, football coach (1908–1973)*

Difficult times are a test of strength. Being able to survive a difficult situation is evidence of strength.

If you're in a difficult situation, don't feel bad about yourself. Instead, see the situation as a chance to show your strength. A difficult situation is simply a challenge and an opportunity to grow stronger.

It is better to practice against a strong team than a weak team. If you win, you'll feel great; however, even if you lose, you will have learned something from the experience. The same is true in business and life in general: bad times push us to be stronger and to work harder. Don't miss these opportunities to show how tough you really are. You might even surprise yourself!

ಐ 13 ಐ

You play to win the game

— *Herman Edwards, football player & coach (1954–)*

If you're not playing to win, why are you playing? If you are not trying your hardest, why try at all? Playing is fun, but it is the goal of winning that makes a game what it is. Winning isn't only about sports. You can often hear Americans say "life is a game."

Of course, winning "the game of life" means different things to different people. It doesn't have to mean making the most money or earning the highest position. Winning can mean whatever you want it to mean, so long as you set goals and work to achieve them. It is important to decide what winning means to you. Then, once you've decided, go after what you want!

14

If you can't beat 'em, join 'em

— *proverb*

If you're on the losing side, take a look at the winners. They must be doing something right. It would be a good idea to learn from them. It might even be a good idea to work with them—to join them. Don't be so stubborn as to miss a chance to learn something or to get ahead.

A Wow, you look nice. Did you get a haircut?

B Yeah. The suit is new, too.

A Since when did you start caring about the way you look?

B I don't care about the way I look. But I've noticed that women pay more attention to guys who care about the way they look.

A Ah, I get it. *If you can't beat 'em, join 'em.*

B Exactly!

15

There is no substitute for hard work

— *Thomas Edison, inventor (1847–1931)*

Hard work is always an important part of success. This is true no matter how talented, attractive, rich, or popular you are. It's not what you are born with, but how you use it that really matters.

It is easy to look at a famous athlete and think: "He is successful because he has natural talent." You might say something similar about a famous actress: "She is successful because she is beautiful." However, talent and beauty are only a part of success. Even naturally talented athletes and beautiful actresses have to work hard. Talent doesn't mean a baseball player doesn't have to practice. Beauty doesn't mean that an actress doesn't have to remember her lines.

Talent and beauty can help you get ahead, but they aren't everything. Hard work is always neccessary.

16

The early bird catches the worm

— *proverb*

When you see an opportunity, act quickly. If you wait too long, someone else will get it before you. This is especially true in the fast-moving world of business. It can also be true in love: if you wait too long to tell someone how you feel, you might lose your chance.

In America, you might see restaurants selling "early bird specials." It doesn't mean they are selling worms! It's a special low price for customers who eat early, usually between 4 p.m. and 6 p.m., before the restaurant becomes busy.

A Did you hear that Linda is leaving the company? That means a new senior management position will be opening up…

B I've already handed in my resume.

A That was fast!

B You know what they say, *the early bird catches the worm.*

17

Success is getting what you want; happiness is wanting what you get

— *Andrew Carnegie, industrialist (1835–1919)*

What does success mean to you? Does it mean money or a job at a famous company? Does it mean living in a particular neighborhood or driving a particular type of car? Will getting those things actually make you happy?

Think about the things—and people—that really do make you happy. Are these the same things that you think about when you think about success? If so, you can think of yourself as lucky! If not, maybe you need to change your ideas about success. Success and happiness should go together. For this to happen, you need to have a clear idea of what makes you happy—and a clear idea of how to get it.

༄ 18 ༅

The squeaky wheel gets the grease

— proverb

Imagine walking into a café on a cold day. You order a hot chocolate to warm up. However, when the hot chocolate arrives, it isn't very hot at all. What do you do? Do you drink the hot chocolate, even though it isn't hot? Or do you complain and ask for another one, one that is actually hot enough to warm you up?

If you don't complain, you won't get what you want. If you do complain, you will.

The wheel that is making noise will get the grease that it needs. The person who speaks up gets what he or she wants. If you want something, you have to let people know that you want it. If you don't tell someone, how will they know?

19

Actions speak louder than words

— proverb

What you do has more power than what you say. Use actions instead of words when you really want someone to notice you.

Here's an example: Joe and Amy are friends. Joe likes Amy, but Amy doesn't know it. Joe often says nice things to Amy. He tells her that she is kind and pretty. But Amy really is kind and pretty, so lots of people tell her this. When Joe says it, Amy doesn't even notice. One day Joe decides to send Amy flowers. Now she notices him! Now she knows that he likes her.

Since actions do get noticed though, be extra careful with what you do. Once you've done something, you can't undo it.

കാ 20 ଦ

There are no gains without pains (No pain, no gain)

— *Ben Franklin, author (1706–1790)*

These days the shorter saying, "no pain, no gain," is more common than Ben Franklin's original expression.

"No pain, no gain" is particularly popular in the sports world. Athletes often practice so hard that their whole body hurts. However, this practice has a purpose: it is supposed to make them stronger, better players. Unless they feel this pain, the coach may say, they are not practicing hard enough.

People use this saying in ordinary life, too. Sometimes if you want to succeed, you have to push yourself hard. This could mean staying up all night to study or working long after it is time to go home. Just remember that there is a limit!

A I think I need to rest.
B We're almost finished. You can do it!
A I don't know…
B Come on! *No pain, no gain*, right?
A Okay. I'll try.

ಐ 21 ೧೪

If a thing is worth doing, it's worth doing well

— *proverb*

If you are going to take the time and energy to do something, do it well. Do the best that you can. If you're not going to do it well, why do it at all? Doing something poorly is a waste of time and energy. Do a thing well so that you can be proud of it.

- **A** Have you finished practicing the piano already?
- **B** I practiced for half an hour. I'll practice more tomorrow.
- **A** Don't you like playing the piano?
- **B** I do like it…
- **A** Then you should keep practicing. *If a thing is worth doing, it's worth doing well.*

22

If you can dream it, you can do it

— *Walt Disney, filmmaker & businessman (1901–1966)*

People used to say "the sky is the limit." This meant that anything on Earth was possible. People used to dream about airplanes. Now they really exist. Now we also have rockets. Clearly the sky is no longer the limit. Now the whole universe is open to us.

Don't limit yourself to what you think is possible. What is possible is always changing. The dreams of ordinary people are largely responsible for this change. Let yourself dream. Let your dreams open your mind to a whole different world—a world where anything is possible. Then think about how you can turn your dreams into reality.

23

Two heads are better than one

— proverb

Two people working together will do a better job than just one person working alone. This is because every person has his or her own strong points and weak points. One person's weak point may be the other person's strong point. Two people working together will have the shared strong points of both people. Having two people work together also means having more ideas.

Having two people work together is a good thing. Having lots of people work together can create problems. This is because there will be too many different ideas and different personalities. There is another proverb to describe this situation: "Too many cooks spoil the soup."

A Do you need any help?

B Sure, that would be great. *Two heads are better than one.*

24

Strike while the iron is hot

— *proverb*

This is your chance to do something, so don't miss it. Act now, or you may not have the chance to act again.

It is often said that "timing is everything." A good plan may fail because it is introduced at the wrong time. An ordinary plan might succeed, just because the timing is right. Unfortunately timing is usually out of your control. The right timing may come before you are ready for it or when you don't expect it. Always be prepared so that you can act when the right time comes.

A Did you talk to the boss about your raise?

B No, not yet.

A He's in a really good mood today. You should talk to him.

B I don't know. I haven't thought about what to say yet…

A He's not in a good mood very often. I'd *strike while the iron is hot* and talk to him now.

25

There's always room at the top

— *Daniel Webster, lawyer & politician (1782–1852)*

Daniel Webster was one of the most famous lawyers in American history. A young law student once complained to him that there were no good jobs for young people. To this Webster replied, "There's always room at the top."

Webster's advice is this: If you are the best at what you do, there will always be a job for you. The best way to make sure that you will have a job is to become very good at what you do. Aim for the top. Even if you don't make it, you will have tried your hardest.

A I'm going to study law.

B Really? There are already too many lawyers. Aren't you worried about finding a job?

A Not at all. *There's always room at the top.*

Love & Friendships

26

Don't judge a book by its cover

— *proverb*

What you see is not always what you get. Book covers can look boring or interesting, but you won't know the truth about the book until you read it. Glasses can make a person look smart. A rich man may wear simple clothes. A sad person may laugh and smile. You can't really know people just by looking at them. Inside, they could be completely different.

A Did you see the new guy?

B Yeah. He looks really serious.

A Have you talked to him?

B No, not yet. But have you noticed that he never smiles?

A Maybe he's just shy. *Don't judge a book by its cover.*

B Yeah, you're right. Have you talked to him?

A No, I haven't either. Let's go introduce ourselves now.

27

Never mix business with pleasure

— *proverb*

It is better to keep relationships and work separate. Mixing the two—even though you might really want to—can lead to trouble.

Here's a common situation: there is a good-looking man or woman in your office. You want to get to know him or her, right? Maybe you start dating. At first things go well, but eventually you start fighting and break up. Now you never want to see that person again. The only problem is, you work in the same office so you'll have to meet every day. This stressful situation will likely affect your ability to work.

The other way around isn't a good idea either: friends and couples who start working together often have problems. Fights about money or ideas create negative feelings that can hurt relationships.

28

There are plenty of fish in the sea

— *proverb*

There are plenty of opportunities out there for romance. Don't feel too bad when one relationship ends. There is always a chance for another relationship and hopefully the next one will work out better. You have to keep looking for the right person. Just remember to watch out for sharks.

A I miss Alex so much! I can't stop thinking about him.

B You just need to meet someone new. That will help you get over him.

A But I'll never meet anyone as good as Alex.

B Sure you will. *There are plenty of fish in the sea*. Just get out there and start looking.

29

Understanding is a two-way street

— *Eleanor Roosevelt, First Lady & activist (1884–1962)*

Understanding must go both ways in order to be true understanding.

If you want someone to understand you, then you must try to understand that person, too. If you want someone to listen to you, then you must listen to him or her in return. If you want people to respect your opinions, then you must respect their opinions. This is true even if your opinions are different from theirs.

People have different personalities and opinions, which can be hard to understand. It is easy to think: "how can somebody be like that?" Or: "how can somebody actually think like that?" However, another person might think the same way about you!

Try to understand why somebody thinks or feels a particular way. Hopefully, in return, he or she will do the same for you.

ಇ 30 ಅ

It takes two to tango

— *proverb*

Tango, like most kinds of dance, needs two people. Many other things in life also need two people, like friendship and romance for example.

It also takes two people to fight. When you find yourself in a fight, don't put all the blame on the other person. Both people in a fight are responsible. Think about what you could have done differently to prevent the fight from happening. Think about what you can say to stop the fight from continuing. A fight can only continue if you allow it to continue.

A Stop it! I don't want to hear anymore. Why are you always shouting at me?

B Hey, *it takes two to tango*. Maybe if you listened to me more, then I wouldn't have to shout.

31

Love is blind

— *proverb*

Love makes an ordinary person appear wonderful. Love can even make an ordinary person appear perfect. This is because people in love often only see the good side of the person they love. They often don't see the bad. People in love see only what they want to see.

Usually it is a good thing that love is blind. After all, nobody is perfect! If love weren't blind, none of us would be loved at all. On the other hand, love can also be dangerous. Love can make people do things that they wouldn't normally do.

A What does she see in him?
B I have no idea. *Love is blind.*

32

Time heals all wounds

— proverb

With time, even a heart that is broken will heal.

When you feel bad, it is hard to imagine that you will ever feel better. However, with time you will feel better. As time goes by, the pain will become less and less. The deeper the wound, the more time it may take. Just be patient and let time do its work.

Do you remember your first broken heart? Was it last year? Five years ago? Twenty years ago? At the time, it must have hurt a lot. Maybe you thought you would never fall in love again! However, with each passing year it hurts less and less. If it happened a long time ago, maybe it doesn't hurt at all now.

Each time someone breaks your heart, it hurts all over again. Remember that with time, your heart will heal again, just as it did in the past.

33

It is not fair to ask of others what you are unwilling to do yourself

— *Eleanor Roosevelt, First Lady & activist (1884–1962)*

If you don't want to do something, then other people probably don't want to do it either. If something is difficult for you to do, it is probably difficult for someone else to do, too.

It is easy to think: "He is stronger than me, so he can do it." Or: "She is more confident than I am, so I'll ask her to do it." However, that person may not be as strong or as confident as he or she appears to be. It might not be as easy as you think for that person to do the thing that you asked.

Think about how you would feel if someone asked you to do the same thing. Would you want to say "no"? Would you be able to say "no"? Asking someone to do something can put that person in a difficult situation. Imagine yourself in the same situation before asking someone to do something.

34

Treat others the way you would like to be treated

— *proverb*

This proverb is called the "golden rule." Children in America usually learn it on their first day of school. It is called the "golden rule," the teacher says, because it is the most important rule in the world.

For children, the message is simple: if you don't want someone to hit you, don't hit other people. If you don't want to be shouted at, don't shout at other people. If you don't want someone to say mean things about you, then don't say mean things about other people.

Adults, on the other hand, seem to have forgotten the message. Too often we make up excuses or blame other people instead of taking responsibility for our actions. Next time you feel yourself about to do something unkind, remind yourself of the "golden rule."

35

Let sleeping dogs lie

— *proverb*

Don't cause trouble. Don't argue about something that happened in the past. Leave the past in the past. Don't bring the past into the present where it can cause trouble again. The noisy dogs have finally gone to sleep. Don't wake them up again!

If talking about something will cause more trouble than staying quiet, it is better to stay quiet.

A I can't believe you got us lost again!

B We're not lost. We just need to…

A That's what you said in Rome! Don't you remember? We walked for hours in the rain and then it started to get dark…

B Why did you have to bring that up now? Can't you just *let sleeping dogs lie*?

ॐ 36 ॐ

If you look for the bad in people, you'll surely find it

— *Abraham Lincoln, President (1809–1865)*

Every person has a good side and a bad side. If you look for the good side, you can easily find it. If you look for the bad side, you can easily find that, too.

Your own attitudes and opinions affect how you see other people. Do you think people are generally good or generally bad? How quickly do you make up your mind about someone? If someone acts badly once, do you think he or she is a bad person? If someone acts badly, do you expect that he or she will always act badly?

Often people see what they expect to see. If you expect to see the good, then that is what you will see. If you expect to see the bad, then that is what you will see. Look for the good in people if that is what you want to see.

Absence makes the heart grow fonder

— *proverb*

Spend time away from the person you love, and you will love him or her more.

It can be difficult to spend a lot of time with someone. The more time you spend with someone, the more you will see his or her bad side. There will be little things that he or she says or does that make you angry. After all, nobody is perfect! Sometimes the bad can make us forget about the good.

However, when the person is gone, memories of the good come back. When you miss someone, you remember all the good things about him or her. This is why it is important for couples to spend some time apart.

A I miss Bob!

B I thought you were mad at him.

A I was. But now that I haven't seen him in a week, I miss him!

B So are you going to forgive him?

A Definitely.

B *Absence really does make the heart grow fonder*, doesn't it?

38

If you can't say anything nice, don't say anything at all

— *proverb*

If you have to choose between saying something unkind and saying nothing, say nothing. If saying something nice would be a lie, then say nothing instead.

Parents teach their children this because they want their children to be polite. However, this proverb is sometimes used to be anything but polite! It can be used to give an honest opinion indirectly. For example, two friends might have a conversation like this:

A What do you think of my new hairstyle?

B Hmm… My mom always told me that *if you can't say anything nice, don't say anything at all.*

So what the person is really saying is: "I can't say anything about your hairstyle because I can't say anything nice about it—because I don't like it at all."

39

Two's company, three's a crowd

— *proverb*

When it comes to romance or close friends, two is the natural number. A third person can feel strange or out of place. When two people seem to like each other, it is best to leave them alone. You don't want to get in the way of a romance.

A What are you doing tonight?
B Oh, Lisa and I are going to go to the movies.
A I haven't seen a movie in a long time. Mind if I join you?
B Sorry. I'm afraid *three's a crowd*.
A Oh, I see! I hope you two have a good time.

40

Misery loves company

— proverb

People who are unhappy look for other people who are unhappy.

Someone who has problems often wants to talk about his or her problems. Someone in a difficult situation may want to complain about it. However, that person needs a listener—someone to listen to the talking and complaining. The best listener is another unhappy person. When two unhappy people get together, they can complain about their problems to each other.

Sometimes you have an unhappy friend who wants to talk to you about his or her problems. Maybe he or she wants advice. Of course you should support your friend. However, be careful that his or her unhappy feelings don't spread to you. When one person starts complaining, it is easy for another to start complaining, too.

ఇ 41 ఞ

Knowledge speaks, but wisdom listens

— *Jimi Hendrix, musician (1942–1970)*

Smart people speak; even smarter people listen. Through speaking, you can share what you know with other people. Through listening, you can learn from others. Only through listening can you get new knowledge, so listening can actually make you smarter.

Everybody knows how much Americans love to talk. Often in America it seems like everyone just wants to be heard and no one wants to listen. That's why advice like this is necessary. It reminds us that sometimes the best thing you can do in a situation is to keep your mouth closed. Of course not everyone wants to listen to this advice!

42

Good fences make good neighbors

— *proverb*

A fence marks the line in between two houses. A good, strong fence will keep noise, dogs, and baseballs on the side where they belong. It will stop the children next door from picking apples from the neighbor's tree. Having a fence means that two families can live side by side and still have their own space. The less neighbors fight over little things—like whose dog went into whose garden—the more they like each other.

Fences draw a clear line between what belongs to one person and what belongs to another. The clearer these lines are, the less there is to argue about. This is true not just among neighbors but also among friends and co-workers.

43

Good friends are hard to find

— *proverb*

The difference between a friend and a good friend is huge. A friend is someone who comes to your birthday party when you invite him or her. A good friend is someone who always remembers your birthday without having to be told. A friend is someone whom you can meet for coffee and talk about many things. A good friend is someone with whom you can talk about everything. A good friend is someone who will be there for you no matter what happens.

Good friends are a lot harder to find than ordinary friends. When times are difficult, it is easy to understand who your good friends really are. They are the ones who offer their support. Count yourself lucky to have these people in your life—they are rare.

Human Nature

44

The grass is always greener on the other side of the fence

— *proverb*

Your neighbor has a nicer car than you. Your best friend often travels to foreign countries for work. If only you could have a nicer car. If only you could travel to foreign countries more often. Then, maybe you would be happier.

On the other hand, your neighbor hates his car because it uses too much gas. He wishes that he had your car. Maybe your friend is tired of traveling. She wants to spend more time at home.

What you don't have often looks better than what you do have. That doesn't mean it is better. Stop wishing for something else and be happy with what you have. Also, stop looking over the neighbor's fence.

∞ 45 ∞

Hindsight is always 20-20

— *Billy Wilder, filmmaker (1906–2002)*

Hindsight is the view of the past from the position of the present. 20-20 vision is perfect vision. It is much easier to understand clearly what happened in the past than to see clearly what is happening in the present.

After a relationship has finished, it is easy to understand what you did right and what you did wrong. You can see which decisions changed your relationship for the better or for the worse. You can look back and realize what was really important and what wasn't. It is hard to see this from the present, particularly because you don't know what will happen in the future.

Often people make mistakes that they don't realize. Sometimes they fail to understand what their partner wants or needs. Only later do they understand what they should have done. The only problem is that it is often too late.

෨ 46 ෨

Nobody is perfect

— *proverb*

Everybody makes mistakes. No matter how hard you try to be perfect, it is only natural that you will make mistakes sometimes. Even though you make mistakes, you still hope to be loved and forgiven, right? In return, try to love and forgive others even when they make mistakes.

Don't expect someone to be perfect, no matter how badly you want him or her to be! When it comes to relationships between people, you cannot take the good without some of the bad.

- **A** I've been waiting for half an hour!
- **B** I'm sorry. Work finished late. I got here as fast as I could.
- **A** You could have called.
- **B** I already said I was sorry. Come on, *nobody's perfect*. Are you going to stay mad at me all night?
- **A** Maybe.

ns 47 ca

Old habits die hard

— *proverb*

Habits, especially bad habits, are hard to break. The older the habit is, the harder it is to break.

Even though it might be hard to break a habit, people still try. At least people often say they are going to try. That doesn't mean that they will actually succeed. Will someone who has smoked for 40 years really be able to quit? Of course, people can change and sometimes they do. We should be happy and surprised if they do; however, we shouldn't expect people to change just because they say they are going to change.

A I ran into Joe last weekend at a bar.
B What? I thought he had given up drinking.
A You know what they say, *old habits die hard.*

෨ 48 ෬

Nice guys finish last

— Leo Durocher, baseball manager (1906–1991)

Actually Leo Durocher didn't say these exact words. He said that a team had nice players, but that they were in last place. A clever newspaper editor changed his original sentence into this famous headline. Even though the words weren't correct, they quickly became popular. Such is the power of the media!

But is it true? Do nice guys really finish last? It often seems that in work and in relationships, nice guys can't win. In business, being nice can make you look weak. In relationships, women say they want a nice guy but often choose a bad one instead.

If it is true, however, it is because we make it true. If you don't want the nice guys to finish last, give them more respect. Make sure they don't always finish last!

49

Beauty is only skin deep

— *proverb*

Beauty is only what you see on the surface. A beautiful outside does not mean a beautiful inside. Someone may be attractive, but he or she also may be unkind. On the other hand, someone who isn't attractive may be a wonderful person! It's the whole person that counts—and the skin is only a small part of the whole person. The more time you spend with someone, the more this becomes true.

A Have you met Joe's new girlfriend? She's really beautiful.

B Yeah. But have you spent any time with her? She's so boring—no personality at all. If I were him, I wouldn't be able to stand it.

A Really? That's too bad. I guess it's true what people say about *beauty being only skin deep*.

50

Man cannot live on bread alone

— *proverb*

Men—and women, too!—need basic things to survive. We need air to breathe, water to drink, food to eat, and a house to protect us from the sun and rain. However, a life with only these basic things would be a sad and lonely one. People also need family and friends; we need music and laughter.

Work is important, but it is not the only important thing in life. Make sure to make time for the other important things. As the actress Marilyn Monroe once famously said: "A career is wonderful, but you can't curl up with it on a cold night."

❧ 51 ☙

A person's a person no matter how small

— *Dr. Seuss, author (1904–1991)*

This line is from a famous children's book. The main point of the book is this: even small people have something to say. Their voices might be small, but that means we should try extra hard to hear them. What's more, many small people can come together to make one big voice. Then they can be noisy.

But what does it mean to be a "small person"? In this case, small doesn't mean short. It means someone who is often ignored. It could be someone who is so poor or so young that people don't listen seriously to what he or she says. However these "small people" are people, too! We should give them the same respect that we give the "big people."

52

The apple doesn't fall far from the tree

— *proverb*

It is not surprising that children follow what their parents do. Just as apples come from trees, children come from their parents. They will have many things in common, even after the children grow up and move away. The seeds from the apple will grow into new trees, and the pattern will continue.

This isn't the only proverb that compares people to apples. Another one is "one bad apple spoils the whole bunch." This means that one bad person in the group can make the whole group look bad.

A Did your daughter decide what she wants to study?

B She's going to study science like her dad.

A *The apple doesn't fall far from the tree*, does it?

B Not in her case! My son, on the other hand…

53

Hunger is the best sauce

— *proverb*

Nothing tastes as good as it does when you're hungry. Even the most ordinary food will taste extraordinary to someone who really needs it. On the other hand, to someone who is not hungry, the same food won't taste as good. It might even taste bad! Desire has a taste of its own. Cooks may spend years studying how to make perfect sauces; however, hunger is the one ingredient they can't control.

A I think this is the best hamburger I've ever eaten.

B You're just saying that because we've been walking for hours and haven't eaten anything all day.

A Maybe so. In that case, *hunger is the best sauce*.

54

Most people are about as happy as they make their minds up to be

— *Abraham Lincoln, President (1809–1865)*

It is often said that "happiness is a state of mind." By simply choosing to be happy, you can actually become happy.

Do you usually see the bad side of a situation? Do you get angry or sad over small things? If you answered "yes" to either question, you might not be as happy as you could be. The good news is that you can change. Choose to see the good in a situation instead of the negative. Choose to forgive and forget small things instead of getting angry. By making these small changes, you can choose to be happier.

There are a lot of things beyond your control. Don't give up control over the one important thing you can control—your attitude.

55

One man's trash is another man's treasure

— *proverb*

Things have different value for different people. This is because different people have different needs. One person puts an old piece of furniture out on the street because he doesn't need it. To him, it's trash. Another person, who does need it, picks it up and takes it home. To him, it's treasure. Just because you don't want something doesn't mean that nobody wants it.

A What's in all these bags?

B Oh, just some old clothes that I never wear. I'm going to throw them out.

A Can I have a look? I could use some new clothes for work.

B Sure. But everything in there is really old.

A *One man's trash is another man's treasure*! Hey, this shirt is nice. Can I have it?

B Take anything you want.

56

You are as old as you think you are

— *Muhammad Ali, athlete (1942–)*

How old are you? How old do you feel? Age is just a number. It is the number of years that you have been alive. How old you feel depends on your own attitude and experience.

Someone who has had many life experiences may feel older than people who are the same age. Someone who has less experience may feel younger. On the other hand, someone who has a lot of energy will also feel younger, even if he or she is in fact quite old. What's more, the same person can feel either young or old, depending on his or her mood.

How old you feel also depends on what you think it means to be "old." Maybe when you were ten years old, you thought twenty was "old." However, once you become twenty or forty, it doesn't feel as old as you thought it would.

Good Advice

57

Don't count your chickens before they've hatched

— *proverb*

You've got eggs, but that doesn't mean that they'll turn into chickens. Success is never certain until it actually happens. Wait until you know for sure, then start counting and making plans.

A How did your presentation go?

B Great. My boss was very happy with it.

A Hey, that's great to hear!

B I'm thinking that, if all goes well, I should finally be able to get that promotion. I can picture it already: a corner office, my name on the door...

A Be careful. *Don't count your chickens before they've hatched.*

B Yeah, I know. But I can dream, can't I?

58

If you don't like the heat, get out of the kitchen

— *proverb*

Kitchens get hot. If you work in one, you are going to sweat. If you don't like to sweat, then you shouldn't work in a kitchen.

This isn't just about being a cook, though. Any high-pressure job is going to make you sweat. There will be stress, responsibility, and competition. If you can't handle these pressures, then maybe you should work in a job that doesn't have them.

Of course many of the most attractive jobs come with a lot of stress. Before choosing a career, think long and hard about what job best matches your personality and abilities. If you do choose a high-pressure job, don't complain about it—after all, it was your choice. If the stress becomes too much for you, maybe you should look for a different job.

59

Don't bite off more than you can chew

— *proverb*

Don't try to do too much at once. Be realistic about what you can and cannot do. Don't accept a task if you don't have the skills for it. Don't accept a role if you don't have the time for it—even if that role is very attractive! Think about the other responsibilities you already have. It is better to finish one thing before moving on to the next.

If you attempt to do too much, then maybe you won't be able to complete anything. If you agree to do something that is too difficult for you, you may not be able to do a good job. It is important to have a clear understanding of your abilities and to make realistic decisions.

60

Money doesn't grow on trees

— *proverb*

Be careful with your money. It is not easily replaced.

If only there were such a thing as a money tree! You could plant it in your garden and have a steady supply of money. Unfortunately, there is no such thing. Money doesn't come that easily to most people. Most people have to work for it. Also, the jobs and family members that provide us with money may not always be around. It is important to keep this in mind when you spend money.

- **A** Hey mom, can I have $50?
- **B** I just gave you $50 yesterday. What happened to that money?
- **A** I spent it already.
- **B** You spend money too quickly. *It doesn't grow on trees*, you know.

61

Quit while you're ahead

— proverb

So long as you're winning, you should keep playing, right? After all, the more you play, the more you can win. The trouble is, you have to keep winning. You never know when your luck will run out. You might win the next game or you might lose. You might lose terribly and lose everything. It is safer to quit while you're ahead than to keep playing until you lose.

The time to quit an argument is when you are winning. If you keep fighting, you might find yourself on the losing side. The time to finish a relationship is before things get too ugly. If things don't get too ugly, you might be able to stay friends.

Everything we do in life is a gamble. We don't know how things will turn out in the end. It is important to look for signs that your luck might change. That is the time to think about making a decision—before it is too late.

62

Don't bite the hand that feeds you

— proverb

If you depend on someone, don't treat that person badly. If you do, he or she may not support you anymore.

This proverb is a favorite of parents. When children get angry and shout at their parents, they are likely to hear their mom or dad say "don't bite the hand that feeds you."

This saying is not just for children, though. Adults depend on their jobs so they shouldn't say or do something unkind towards their bosses—at least not in front of them.

   A I don't care what you say! I'm going out.

   B No, you're not. Get back here.

   A You're the meanest mom in the world.

   B I *wouldn't bite the hand that feeds you*, if I were you. As long as you live in this house, you live under my rules.

   A I'm so tired of hearing that.

   B Someday, when you're a parent, you'll understand.

63

People in glass houses shouldn't throw stones

— *proverb*

A glass house is weak. Anyone can throw a stone and easily break it. If you live in a glass house, you don't want people to throw stones at you. If you throw a stone at someone else, then he or she is likely to throw a stone back at you. If that happens, your glass house will be in trouble. To protect yourself, you shouldn't start throwing stones.

Of course people don't live in glass houses; a glass house is too weak. However, people have many other weak points. We all have weak points. If you don't want someone to attack your weak points, then don't attack that person's weak points. The best way to protect yourself from getting hurt is to avoid hurting others.

∞ 64 ∞

Don't burn your bridges behind you

— *proverb*

If you burn the bridge to your past, you can never go back again. Everything you worked for will be lost to you forever.

Imagine you've been offered a new, better job. Finally, you will have the opportunity to work for a company that truly appreciates your talents. Your new job won't start until next month; until then, you'll keep working at your old job. Since you're leaving soon, there is no reason to keep working hard, right? Why not just take it easy for a few weeks?

Sure, a few easy weeks would be nice, but it's not a good idea. You need to keep working hard because you don't know what will happen in the future. Maybe something will go wrong at your new job. Someday you might want to go back to your old company. Someday you may find yourself working with the same people again. For this reason, you don't want to lose the trust of your old company and co-workers.

All that glitters is not gold

— *proverb*

Just because something looks like gold doesn't mean it is gold. Things are not always what they appear to be. Something that appears to be wonderful may not be wonderful at all. Don't be easily fooled!

Fame is a good example. To many of us, fame is very attractive. Famous people wear beautiful clothes, travel around the world, and go to fancy parties. Given the choice, many of us would choose to be famous. However, famous people aren't always happy. They get lonely and sad, too. They might worry that their friends only like them because they are famous. If you start to think about it, fame doesn't sound like real "gold" at all.

66

Be careful what you wish for

— *proverb*

Here's the full sentence: "Be careful what you wish for, you might receive it." Since it is such a famous saying, people just say the first half because everyone knows how it ends.

"Be careful what you wish for" isn't just a famous proverb. It is also the opening line of a famous horror story. In the story a man receives a strange object from an old friend. The friend tells him that the object has the power to make wishes come true. The man makes a wish and it comes true, but not exactly in the way he expected it to. In fact, the wish comes true in a horrible way.

The meaning of the story (and the proverb) is that a wish can be a dangerous thing. Sometimes the thing that you want turns out to be very different from what you imagined. Your wish might come true, but it might also bring you many problems that you didn't have before.

67

What goes around, comes around

— proverb

If you spread gossip about other people, then other people are likely to spread gossip about you. If you hurt other people, then other people are likely to hurt you back. On the other hand, positive words and positive actions should create positive words and positive actions in return.

A Did you hear that Kate stopped talking to Amy?

B No. Why's that?

A Amy really made Kate angry by spending a lot of time with that guy whom Kate likes.

B But didn't Kate do the same thing to Emily a few months ago?

A I know. I don't feel sorry for Kate at all. *What goes around, comes around.* I hope she's learned her lesson!

68

The devil is in the details

— proverb

You've been offered a new job with higher pay. Sounds great, right? You had better check that contract carefully, though. Will you have to work weekends? How many vacation days will you get? How far is the office from your home and will the company pay for your gas or train fare? These small details can actually make a big difference. A great deal can start to look like a bad one once these details come to light.

This shouldn't be a surprise. Often these details are hidden on purpose to make a bad deal look good. That's where the word "devil" comes in; in Western culture, the devil is responsible for making the bad look good. Always check contracts and plans carefully, and when in doubt, ask questions!

69

If it ain't broke, don't fix it

— *Bert Lance, politician (1931–)*

Naturally, we want to make things better. Good is good until we get used to it. Good is good until it gets boring. We want our computers to do more. We want our businesses to earn more. We want our relationships to be more and more exciting. We want so badly to improve things that we forget to be happy that something actually works just fine the way it is.

Sometimes, by trying to make something better, people actually make something worse. A plan to grow a business can result in huge losses instead. A vacation designed to bring two people closer together can end in an argument. If something is working, leave it alone. Instead, put your energy towards the things in your life that really do need fixing.

70

Never say never

— *proverb*

Anything can happen, so don't say that it won't. Of course this can be both a good thing and a bad thing. It's good when something you hoped for, but thought impossible, actually happens. Some good examples would be getting your dream job or finding the perfect partner. Never say never—these things can happen!

It's bad when something you weren't prepared for actually does happen. Just because something seems impossible doesn't mean that it is impossible. It is a good idea to prepare for anything, even the worst possible situation.

- **A** How was your date last night?
- **B** Terrible. I don't think I'll ever find the right man.
- **A** Hey, *never say never*! He's out there somewhere. You just have to keep looking.

Where there is smoke, there is fire

— *proverb*

A bad sign, like smoke, is good evidence that a bad situation, like fire, is coming. Look out for warning signs and don't ignore them if you see them.

If you notice a small problem early, you may be able to keep it from growing into a larger problem. You will have time to prepare. If possible, you may even be able to avoid a bad situation completely. If you ignore the signs, however, you'll have no one to blame but yourself.

A Something's not right at work. Nobody got a raise this year and a lot of people are quitting.

B That doesn't sound good. *Where there's smoke, there's fire.* The company might be in trouble. I'd start looking for a new job, if I were you.

72

Don't put all your eggs in one basket

— proverb

If you put all your eggs in one basket, and the basket gets lost or stolen, you won't have any eggs left. It would be better to have your eggs in several baskets. Then if one gets stolen, you'll still have the eggs in the other baskets.

This proverb isn't really about eggs, though. It's about the choices we make and about preparing for the future. What happens if you can't get the job you want? What happens if you lose the job you have? Do you have other skills that you can use to make money? Where is your money? Is it invested in one place or many?

Life often doesn't go the way we want it to go. Life often doesn't go the way we expect it to go. It is important to prepare for many possible situations by having many "baskets."

73

Better safe than sorry

— proverb

When you have a choice between a safe option and a risky option, choose the safe option. The risky option may look more attractive; however, if it doesn't work out, you could be in trouble. The safer option may look less attractive, but at least you won't have to worry about trouble. Few results are worth the risk of getting into trouble.

A I'm thinking of quitting my job.

B Do you have a new job lined up?

A No, not yet. But I think I should be able to find one. It would be nice to have some time off from working.

B I don't know. I think you should find a new job before you quit your old one. *Better safe than sorry.*

What you don't know can't hurt you

— *proverb*

Sometimes it is better not to know something. Sometimes hearing something can cause pain. Sometimes it is better to hear no news than to hear bad news.

Bad news can make you feel bad, worried, or afraid. Bad news can change your life. If you don't hear bad news, then you won't feel bad. If nobody tells you something bad, then your life can stay the same.

The trouble with information is that once you know it, you can't stop knowing it. As long as you don't know, you can still hope for the best.

A Did you get your test result yet?
B Yeah, it came in the mail yesterday.
A So?
B I don't know. I didn't look at it yet.
A What? Why not?
B *What I don't know can't hurt me.*

lessons for living

75

If life hands you a lemon, make lemonade

— *proverb*

Make the best of your current situation, even if it is not the best situation. With a little creativity, you can turn something sour into something sweet. A little sugar and water are the only difference between lemons and lemonade.

Life gives us many examples of this. A blind child develops an excellent sense of hearing and later become a famous musician. A woman turns her painful divorce into a popular book that sells millions. Find the positive in the negative.

A I heard about the accident. Are you okay?

B Yes, I'll be fine. But my leg is broken. I have to stay in bed for a whole month.

A That's terrible! But look on the bright side: now you'll have time to work on your painting.

B Yeah...

A Hey, stay positive! *When life hands you a lemon, make lemonade.*

B You're right. I should make good use of this time.

∞ 76 ∞

Today is the first day of the rest of your life

— *Abbie Hoffman, activist (1936–1989)*

Do you wish you could change your life? Wouldn't it be nice to start again from the beginning?

Nobody can change the past. However, each day you can change the present. Look forward to the rest of your life. Don't look backwards to the part that you can't change. Yesterday may have been bad, but today can be good. What about the future? It can be great, but only if you start working on the present.

For hundreds of years, people have come to America from other countries to begin a new life. Because of this, Americans feel strongly that a fresh start is possible.

Actually, you don't need to move to have a fresh start; anyone can begin a new life anywhere. You just need to make a decision to start fresh. Try looking in the mirror and telling yourself: "Today is the first day of the rest of my life." Then start living the way you want to live.

77

Don't sweat the small stuff

— *proverb*

Don't worry about small problems. If you worry about every little thing, then you won't have enough strength left over to worry about the big problems. It is better to save your energy for when you really need it. More importantly, don't turn small problems into big ones. Stay calm and let things pass.

A Andy said he would call me yesterday, but he didn't. Do you think he doesn't like me? Should I call him?

B *Don't sweat the small stuff.* He was probably just busy. I'm sure he'll call you soon.

A And if he doesn't?

B Then forget about him! Just don't waste time and energy worrying about it, okay?

78

Truth is stranger than fiction

— *Mark Twain, author (1835–1910)*

Books and movies often tell stories that are hard to believe. However, sometimes what happens in real life is even harder to believe. What happens in books and movies is limited to what the author can imagine. In real life, things can happen that we couldn't possibly imagine.

An actor becomes governor of a state. A man who never finished college runs one of the richest companies in the world. Someone puts a video on the Internet and becomes famous in just a few hours. Two people with the same name date the same person. Another gets married and divorced eight times. These things are hard to imagine but have all happened. Life is full of surprises!

79

Practice what you preach

— *proverb*

Follow your own advice. Doctors who tell their patients to exercise should exercise, too. Teachers who teach their students to work hard should work hard, too. If you don't follow your own advice, it is hard for others to take your advice seriously. You can't expect other people to listen to you if you don't listen to yourself. Be the kind of person who inspires other people.

A I heard the boss was sleeping during the meeting this morning.

B What? He's always getting angry with us for doing that. Why doesn't he *practice what he preaches*?

A Because he's the boss.

80

Every cloud has a silver lining

— *proverb*

Clouds block the sun and make the sky dark. Sometimes they bring rain that ruins our plans. However, if you look closely, you can see the light trying to break through around the edges. This part of the cloud isn't gray; it shines like silver.

In every bad situation, there is a small amount of good that shines through, just like the silver part of the cloud. Find this good and you can turn a negative situation into a positive one. You can turn an unhappy experience into a learning experience. The end of a romantic relationship, for example, can mean more time to spend with your friends.

Being positive takes practice. It isn't always easy to find the good when a situation seems so bad. Once you find it though, life looks a lot brighter.

∞ 81 ∞

Either get busy living or get busy dying

— *Stephen King, writer (1947–)*

Sometimes it seems that life is just a pattern of getting up, going to work, eating dinner, watching television, and going back to bed. Is this really living? Shouldn't there be more excitement? Shouldn't there be more joy?

The good things in life don't always happen by themselves. Often, we have to make them happen. Get up early and watch the sunrise. Turn off the TV and take a walk in the park. Get busy doing what makes you happy. If you aren't busy doing the things that make you happy, what are you busy doing? If you don't take control of your life, someone else will—and before you know it, it will be gone.

82

Beggars can't be choosers

— *proverb*

If you need to eat, you can't be picky about the food. Of course, a steak would be better than a slice of bread. But if you're hungry and a slice of bread is the only thing around, you won't say "no" to it. It's the same with jobs; you might want to wait for a better offer, but if you need to work, you'd better take what you can get.

This is advice for times when your luck is bad and few opportunities exist. Hopefully your luck will change and you won't be a "beggar" forever.

A How's your new job?
B Well, it's certainly not my dream job. But in this economy…
A Yeah, I know what you mean. *Beggars can't be choosers.*

83

In the future everyone will be world-famous for fifteen minutes

— *Andy Warhol, artist (1928–1987)*

The artist Andy Warhol said this in 1968. He was saying that society was moving in a direction that would allow anybody—not just people with power—to be famous, if only for a short time.

Warhol didn't live to see the Internet; however, his words certainly seem to describe our present world. Today anybody can post something to the Internet and be famous, if only for a short time.

From this quote, we also get the popular saying "my fifteen minutes of fame." For example, you might hear someone say: "She's had her fifteen minutes of fame; when will it be my turn?"

There is no need to be jealous, though. Everyone can have a turn under the spotlight if they want it.

84

You can't have your cake and eat it, too

— *proverb*

If you eat your cake now, you'll have nothing for later. If you save your cake for later, you won't have it to eat now. There is no way to get around this. Once you eat the cake, it is gone forever!

The cake represents the good things in life. Sometimes it is not possible to have two good things at the same time. When this happens, you have to make a choice. It is a hard choice, but remember that either way you are getting a good thing.

- **A** How are things going with Lisa?
- **B** Great. We get along really well. The only thing is that I kind of miss being single. You know, going out and meeting new people…
- **A** So you're saying that *you want to eat your cake and have it too*?
- **B** If only that were possible!

∞ 85 ∞

Wake up and smell the coffee

— *Ann Landers, newspaper columnist (1918–2002)*

Breakfast in America usually starts with a big cup of coffee. The strong smell of coffee wakes up the senses, pulling people from their dreams and preparing them to face the day.

Do you have a friend who seems to live in a dream world? Does he or she often miss important signs? If you think your friend needs to pay more attention to the real world, you might want to remind him or her to "wake up and smell the coffee."

A Have you heard from Jim?

B No. I just don't get it! We had such a good time together last weekend. I've called him three times since then, but he never picks up the phone.

A You called him three times already? I wouldn't have called more than once.

B Really?

A *Wake up and smell the coffee*, Kate. If he didn't call you back yet, he's probably not going to call you back.

86

Better late than never

— *proverb*

Naturally, we want things when we want them. We want food when we are hungry. We want an apology from a friend when he or she hurts us. We want a great job when we are looking for one. Of course, things don't always turn out the way we want. Sometimes what we want takes a lot longer to arrive than we would have liked. Instead of complaining about the timing, however, just be happy that you finally got what you wanted!

A My brother finally paid me back. It took him two years!

B Hey, *better late than never*. At least you got the money.

87

Anyone who has never made a mistake has never tried anything new

— *Albert Einstein, scientist (1879–1955)*

If you try something new, you will probably make a mistake. This is only natural if you are doing something for the first time. It's okay to make mistakes in the beginning because this is how you learn. Sometimes it is necessary to make many mistakes before you get it right. That's okay, too. The important thing is to learn from the mistakes.

If you aren't making mistakes, then you aren't challenging yourself. A challenge can appear scary, but it doesn't need to be. A challenge is an opportunity to learn and gain new skills. Through challenges we can also gain experience and confidence. Ask yourself which is better: trying something new and making a mistake or never trying anything new at all?

88

What doesn't kill you only makes you stronger

— *proverb*

To be alive is the most important thing in life. As long as you are alive, you can work on improving your situation.

With every difficult situation that you survive, you grow stronger. Most likely you are stronger than you realize! Situations that seemed terrible in the past may seem easier now because you have grown stronger. People who have lived through many terrible situations become very strong.

A I can't believe he left me! What am I going to do? I have no job, no money...

B It's terrible, I know! But you will be okay. You can't give up. Remember, *what doesn't kill you only makes you stronger.*

A Well then, if I survive this, I'm going to be very strong. He'd better watch out!

෴ 89 ෴

Showing up is 80 percent of life

— *Woody Allen, filmmaker (1935–)*

You may not be the best at what you do. You may not have been the smartest kid in the class or the fastest on the team. You may be completely ordinary and average. Don't feel bad about yourself! Being smart or fast can make you a success, but not if you can't get out of bed in the morning.

Ordinary skills, such as getting out of bed and getting dressed in the morning, really matter more than we think they do. Without these skills, nothing would get done! The simple act of showing up and getting to work on time is the starting point for everything else.

90

There is no free lunch

— *Harley L. Lutz, economist (1882–1975)*

Few gifts are true gifts; most have to be repaid at some point.

Be careful of the friend who invites you to lunch. She may ask you for a favor. Be careful of the neighbor who offers you the extra vegetables from his garden. Go over there to pick them up and you'll spend an hour listening to his problems. Be extra careful of the man who treats you to an expensive meal!

A free lunch may sound like a good idea, but remember that you'll likely have to pay for it some other way. Money is not the only currency and not always the most valuable one; time, energy, and attention can be just as valuable.

91

It doesn't rain but it pours

— proverb

When one bad thing happens, many bad things happen. Maybe this is true; maybe it isn't. However, it seems to be true! Bad luck seems to bring more bad luck. Or maybe it is just easier to see the bad—especially when something bad has just happened.

On the other hand, sometimes one good thing brings more good things. Sometimes it can bring more good things than you really want or need. Here's an example: John is looking for a job. Many months go by, but he still can't find a job. Suddenly he gets a job offer, then another, then another. Now he has too many job offers and has to make a difficult decision. In this situation John is probably thinking, "It doesn't rain but it pours."

92

A penny saved is a penny earned

— *Ben Franklin, writer (1706–1790)*

Saving a penny is the same as earning one. A penny is a penny; it doesn't make any difference to your wallet how it got there.

Of course, a penny doesn't sound like much money these days. Save a penny a day, and in a year, all you can buy yourself is a sandwich. However, start thinking about dollars and the numbers add up a lot quicker. Think about how small amounts of money quickly disappear—on taxi rides and cups of coffee, for example. Before spending money on these things, think about whether or not you really need them.

If you can save a few dollars every day, then in a year, you may be able to afford a vacation. Now that is something worth working for! What's more, the more money you save, the less you have to work for what you want.

93

Control your own destiny, or someone else will

— *Jack Welch, businessman (1935–)*

Life is full of choices. If you don't make them yourself, then somebody else will make them for you.

How many choices in your life have you made on your own? How many did you let others make? How many choices did you avoid making, because it was easier that way?

Making choices can be difficult. Sometimes there are too many options to choose from. Sometimes there aren't enough good options. Sometimes you don't want to feel responsible for making a difficult decision.

However difficult, making your own choices can put you in control of your own life. A sense of control can give you more confidence.

94

You don't need a weatherman to tell which way the wind blows

— *Bob Dylan, musician (1941–)*

You don't need an expert—or a machine!—to tell you what you can understand by yourself.

In the past, people used to tell time by checking the sun. Now we use clocks. That's not to say that clocks are bad; in fact, they're very useful for measuring time exactly. However, by using clocks, we've lost the ability to tell time by the sun. Most of us would probably turn on the TV to check the weather instead of opening the window.

Listen to your body. Your senses can tell you a lot more than you realize. What we learn in school and in books is only one kind of information. Real experience offers another kind of information that is just as valuable.

95

When in Rome, do as the Romans do

— *proverb*

When you travel outside your own culture, follow the customs of the local people. Follow the local customs even if these customs are different from your own. Eat something that you have never eaten before, even if it looks strange. Find out what the local people are excited about—a festival or a sports event maybe—and join in.

Trying new things is part of the experience of traveling. You may have the chance to try something that doesn't even exist in your culture. You might even discover that you like something that you didn't think you would. Sometimes you even get to do something that isn't allowed in your own culture.

96

The only thing we have to fear is fear itself

— *Franklin D. Roosevelt, President (1882–1945)*

Roosevelt said this famous line in 1933. At the time, the economy in America was very bad. People were afraid. They were afraid of losing their jobs. If they had already lost their jobs, they were worried about losing their homes. They were afraid that things would never get better.

People had good reasons to be afraid. Maybe the economy would only get worse; on the other hand, maybe it would get better. It is important to stay positive and hope for the best. Without hope, it is impossible to imagine a better future. Fear destroys this hope and that is why it is dangerous. Fight back against fear with positive thinking.

97

Do a common thing in an uncommon way

— *Booker T. Washington, educator & author (1856–1915)*

Every day millions of people on Earth do the same things. We get up in the morning, eat breakfast, go to work, and so on. Often, we do the same thing the same way that our parents did and that their parents did before them. We do so many of these common things without even thinking about how or why we do them. We do so many things without thinking that there might be a different or better way to do them.

Since these are things that you do every day, doing just one of those things differently can make a big difference in your life. What's more, doing an ordinary thing in a different way can make people notice you. Doing an ordinary thing in a better way can earn you respect.

98

Reality is something you rise above

— *Liza Minnelli, actress & singer (1946–)*

Reality is what life gives you. You may have been born male or female, tall or short. You may stay healthy or you may get sick. Reality is not always what we would choose, if we had the choice.

However, what you choose to do with what life gives you is up to you. You can choose to accept reality or you can choose to ignore reality. You can also choose to make the best of it.

Reality is only the starting point. See how far you can go from there. Learn to tell the difference between what you think is impossible, what other people tell you is impossible, and what really is impossible.

99

There's no place like home

— *L. Frank Baum, author (1856–1919)*

This is one of the most famous lines from one of the most famous American movies. The movie is "The Wizard of Oz," which was based on the book by L. Frank Baum.

In the story, the main character is taken to a world far away from her home. There are many wonderful things in this world, and she makes some good friends there. However, she really wants to go home, even though her home is just an ordinary home in an ordinary place. Why does she want to go home so badly? Because no place, no matter how wonderful, is as special as home. To get home, she must repeat the words, "There's no place like home."

Maybe you feel the same way after returning home from a holiday. Even though you had a wonderful time, it feels so good to be back in your own house. You open the door, put your bags down, take off your shoes, and think, "There's no place like home!"

∞100∞

The best things in life are free

— *proverb*

Make a list of all of the things that make you happy. How many of the things on that list can be bought? How many of them can't be bought? How many of them are expensive? How many of them are free?

Sure, expensive things can make you happy. However, unless you're rich, you'll have to work hard to be able to buy them. If you need expensive things to be happy, you'll have to work hard your whole life to be happy.

Some important things you can't buy, like love for example. Other examples are a sunny day, a walk in the park, and an afternoon with friends. You can't buy these things, but they can make you just as happy—even happier—than something you can buy. The easiest way to be happy is to enjoy these little free things.

Word List

- LEVEL 1, 2 は本文で使われている全ての語を掲載しています。
  LEVEL 3 以上は、中学校レベルの語を含みません。ただし、本文で特殊な意味で使われている場合、その意味のみを掲載しています。

- 語形が規則変化する語の見出しは原形で示しています。不規則変化語は本文中で使われている形になっています。

- 一般的な意味を紹介していますので、一部の語で本文で実際に使われている品詞や意味と合っていないことがあります。

- 品詞は以下のように示しています。

名 名詞	代 代名詞	形 形容詞	副 副詞	動 動詞	助 助動詞
前 前置詞	接 接続詞	間 間投詞	冠 冠詞	略 略語	俗 俗語
熟 熟語	頭 接頭語	尾 接尾語	号 記号	関 関係代名詞	

A

- **Abbie Hoffman** アビー・ホフマン《政治活動家, 青年国際党 (イッピー) の共同創立者》
- **ability** 名 ①できること, (〜する) 能力 ②才能
- **Abraham Lincoln** エイブラハム・リンカーン《第16代アメリカ合衆国大統領》
- **absence** 名 欠席, 欠如, 不在
- **accept** 動 ①受け入れる ②同意する, 認める
- **accident** 名 ①(不慮の) 事故, 災難 ②偶然
- **achieve** 動 成し遂げる, 達成する, 成功を収める
- **act** 名 行為, 行い 動 ①行動する ②機能する ③演じる
- **activist** 名 活動家
- **actor** 名 俳優, 役者
- **actress** 名 女優
- **actually** 副 実際に, 本当に, 実は
- **add** 動 ①加える, 足す ②足し算をする ③言い添える **add up** 合計する, 計算が合う
- **adult** 名 大人, 成人
- **advice** 名 忠告, 助言, 意見
- **affect** 動 ①影響する ②(病気などが) おかす ③ふりをする
- **afford** 動 《can 〜》〜することができる, 〜する (経済的・時間的な) 余裕がある
- **afraid** 熟 **be afraid of** 〜を恐れる, 〜を怖がる **I'm afraid (that)** 残念ながら〜, 悪いけれど〜
- **ah** 間 《驚き・悲しみ・賞賛などを表して》ああ, やっぱり
- **ahead** 熟 **get ahead** 進歩する, うまくいく, 出世する
- **aim** 動 ねらう, 目指す
- **ain't** are not, is not, has not, have not の短縮形
- **airplane** 名 飛行機
- **Albert Einstein** アルベルト・アインシュタイン《ドイツ生まれのユダヤ人理論物理学者》
- **Alex** 名 アレックス《人名》
- **all** 熟 **after all** やはり, 結局 **all day** 一日中, 明けても暮れても **all over** 〜中で, 全体に亘って, 〜の至る所で **not 〜 at all** 少しも [全然] 〜ない **not at all** 少しも〜でない
- **allow** 動 ①許す, 《- … to 〜》…が〜するのを可能にする, …に〜させて

WORD LIST

おく ②与える
- **alone** 熟 leave ~ alone ~をそっとしておく
- **always** 熟 not always 必ずしも~であるとは限らない
- **America** 名 アメリカ《国名・大陸》
- **American** 形 アメリカ(人)の 名 アメリカ人
- **amount** 名 ①量, 額 ②《the -》合計 動 (総計~に)なる
- **Amy** 名 エイミー《人名》
- **and so on** ~など, その他もろもろ
- **Andrew Carnegie** アンドリュー・カーネギー《実業家。「鋼鉄王」と称された》
- **Andy** 名 アンディ《人名》
- **Andy Warhol** アンディ・ウォーホル《画家・版画家・芸術家, ポップアートの旗手》
- **anger** 名 怒り
- **angry** 熟 get angry 腹を立てる
- **Ann Landers** アン・ランダース《コラムニスト, 本名エスター・"イッピー"・ポーリン・フリードマン・レダラー (Esther "Eppie" Pauline Friedman Lederer)》
- **any time** いつでも
- **anybody** 代 ①《疑問文・条件節で》誰か ②《否定文で》誰も(~ない) ③《肯定文で》誰でも
- **anymore** 副 《通例否定文, 疑問文で》今はもう, これ以上, これから
- **anyone** 代 ①《疑問文・条件節で》誰か ②《否定文で》誰も(~ない) ③《肯定文で》誰でも
- **anything but** ~のほかは何でも, 少しも~でない
- **anywhere** 副 どこかへ[に], どこにも, どこへも, どこにでも
- **apart** 副 ①ばらばらに, 離れて ②別にして, それだけで

- **apartment** 名 アパート
- **apology** 名 謝罪, 釈明
- **appealing** 形 魅力的な, 訴求力がある
- **appear** 動 ①現れる, 見えてくる ②(~のように)見える, ~らしい appear to するように見える
- **appreciate** 動 ①正しく評価する, よさがわかる ②価値[相場]が上がる ③ありがたく思う
- **argue** 動 ①論じる, 議論する ②主張する
- **argument** 名 ①議論, 論争 ②論拠, 理由
- **artist** 名 芸術家
- **as** 熟 as ~ as one can できる限り ~ as good as ~も同然で, ほとんど ~ as long as ~する以上は, ~である限りは as to ~に関しては, ~については, ~に応じて see ~ as … ~をと考える so ~ as to … …するほど~で so long as ~する限りは such ~ as … …のような~ such as たとえば~, ~のような the same ~ as [that] …と同じ(ような)~
- **athlete** 名 運動選手
- **attack** 動 ①襲う, 攻める ②非難する ③(病気が)おかす
- **attempt** 動 試みる, 企てる
- **attend** 動 ①出席する ②世話をする, 仕える ③伴う ④《- to ~》~に注意を払う, 専念する, ~の世話をする
- **attention** 名 ①注意, 集中 ②配慮, 手当て, 世話
- **attitude** 名 姿勢, 態度, 心構え
- **attractive** 形 魅力的な, あいきょうのある
- **author** 名 著者, 作家
- **average** 形 平均の, 普通の
- **avoid** 動 避ける, (~を)しないようにする

- **away** 熟 give away ①ただで与える, 贈る, 譲歩する, 手放す ②(素性・正体を)暴露する, 馬脚を現す move away ①立ち去る ②移す, 動かす take away ①連れ去る ②取り上げる, 奪い去る ③取り除く turn away 向こうへ行く, 追い払う, (顔を)そむける, 横を向く

B

- **back** 熟 get back 戻る, 帰る go back to ～に帰る[戻る], ～に遡る, (中断していた作業に)再び取り掛かる pay back 返済する, お返しをする
- **backwards** 副 後方へ, 逆に, 後ろ向きに
- **bad** 熟 bad luck 災難, 不運, 悪運 That's too bad. 残念だ。
- **badly** 副 ①悪く, まずく, へたに ②とても, ひどく
- **bar** 名 酒場
- **base** 名 塁, ベース《野球》 bases are loaded 満塁です
- **baseball** 名 野球
- **based** 形 ～をベース[基礎]にした be based on ～に基づく
- **basic** 形 基礎の, 基本の
- **batter** 名 バッター, 打者
- **battle** 名 戦闘, 戦い
- **beat** 動 ①打つ, 鼓動する ②打ち負かす
- **beauty** 名 美
- **because of** ～のために, ～の理由で
- **bed** 熟 get out of bed 起きる, 寝床を離れる
- **beggar** 名 乞食, 物貰い
- **beginning** 名 初め, 始まり
- **behind** 前 ～の後ろに, ～の背後に
- **belong** 動《 – to 》～に属する, ～のものである
- **Ben Franklin** ベンジャミン・フランクリン《政治家, 外交官, 著述家, 物理学者, 気象学者》
- **Bert Lance** バート・ランス《カーター政権時代の行政管理予算局長》
- **bet** 動 賭ける
- **better** 熟 feel better 気分がよくなる get better (病気などが)良くなる had better ～したほうが身のためだ, ～しなさい
- **beyond** 前 ～を越えて, ～の向こうに
- **Billy Wilder** ビリー・ワイルダー《映画監督, 脚本家, プロデューサー》
- **bit** 名《a –》少し, ちょっと
- **bite** 動 かむ, かじる bite off 食いちぎる
- **blame** 動 とがめる, 非難する 名 ①責任, 罪 ②非難
- **blind** 形 ①視覚障害がある, 目の不自由な ②わからない ③盲目的な
- **blow** 動 (風が)吹く
- **Bob** 名 ボブ《人名》
- **Bob Dylan** ボブ・ディラン《ミュージシャン》
- **Booker T. Washington** ブッカー・T・ワシントン《教育者, 作家》
- **boring** 形 うんざりさせる, 退屈な
- **boss** 名 上司, 親方, 監督
- **break through** ～を打ち破る
- **break up** ばらばらになる, 解散させる
- **breathe** 動 ①呼吸する ②ひと息つく, 休息する
- **bring up** (問題を)持ち出す
- **broken heart** 失意, 失恋
- **bunch** 名 房, 束, 群れ
- **bus** 名 バス
- **businessman** 名 ビジネスマン, 実業家

Word List

- **but** 熟 anything but ~のほかは何でも, 少しも~でない not ~ but … ~ではなくて

C

- **café** 名 コーヒー[喫茶]店, 軽食堂
- **calm** 形 穏やかな, 落ち着いた
- **can** 熟 as ~ as one can できる限り~ Can I ~? ~してもいいですか。
- **cannot** can (~できる)の否定形 (=can not)
- **care about** ~を気に掛ける
- **career** 名 ①(生涯の・専門的な)職業 ②経歴, キャリア
- **careful of** 《be-》~に注意する
- **case** 熟 in that case もしそうなら
- **catch** 動 捕まえる, 捕らえる
- **celebrity** 名 ①有名人, 名士 ②名声
- **certain** 形 ①確実な, 必ず~する ②(人が)確信した ③ある ④いくらかの
- **certainly** 副 確かに, 必ず
- **challenge** 名 ①挑戦 ②難関 動 挑む, 試す
- **character** 名 (小説・劇などの)登場人物
- **check** 動 照合する, 検査する
- **chew** 動 かむ
- **chocolate** 名 チョコレート
- **choice** 名 選択(の範囲・自由), えり好み, 選ばれた人[物]
- **chooser** 名 選択者
- **clear** 形 ①はっきりした, 明白な ②澄んだ
- **clearly** 副 明らかに, はっきりと
- **clever** 形 ①頭のよい, 利口な ②器用な, 上手な
- **closely** 副 ①密接に ②念入りに, 詳しく ③ぴったりと
- **coach** 名 コーチ, 指導者
- **columnist** 名 コラムニスト, 特設欄執筆者
- **come** 熟 come down ~を下りて来る, 田舎へ来る come for ~の目的で来る, ~を取りに来る come in 中にはいる, やってくる, 出回る come on いいかげんにしろ, もうよせ, さあ来なさい come true 実現する
- **common** 熟 in common (with ~) (~と)共通して
- **compare** 動 ①比較する, 対照する ②たとえる
- **compete** 動 ①競争する ②(競技に)参加する ③匹敵する
- **competition** 名 競争, 競合, コンペ
- **complain** 動 不平[苦情]を言う
- **complete** 動 完成させる
- **completely** 副 完全に, すっかり
- **confidence** 名 自信, 確信, 信頼, 信用度
- **confident** 形 自信のある, 自信に満ちた
- **contract** 名 契約(書), 協定
- **control** 動 ①管理[支配]する ②抑制する, コントロールする 名 ①管理, 支配(力) ②抑制 in control ~を支配して, ~を掌握している sense of control コントロール感 take control of ~を制御[管理]する, 支配する
- **conversation** 名 会話, 会談
- **correct** 形 正しい, 適切な, りっぱな
- **cost** 動 (金・費用が)かかる, (~を)要する, (人に金額を)費やさせる
- **could** 熟 could have done ~だったかもしれない《仮定法》If + 《主語》+ could ~できればなあ《仮定法》
- **count** 動 数える
- **couple** 名 ①2つ, 対 ②夫婦, 一組

INSPIRATIONAL PROVERBS AND SAYINGS

- **course** 熟 of course もちろん, 当然
- **cover** 名 覆い, カバー
- **co-worker** 名 同僚, 仕事仲間
- **create** 動 創造する, 生み出す, 引き起こす
- **creativity** 名 創造性, 独創力
- **crowd** 名 群集, 雑踏, 多数, 聴衆
- **curl** 動 カールする, 巻きつく curl up 丸まって横になる, 丸まって寝る
- **currency** 名 通貨, 貨幣
- **current** 形 現在の, 目下の, 通用[流通]している
- **customer** 名 顧客

D

- **Daniel Webster** ダニエル・ウェブスター《政治家, 法律家》
- **dark** 熟 get dark 暗くなる
- **day** 熟 all day 一日中, 明けても暮れても each day 毎日, 日ごとに every day 毎日 every single day 一日も欠かさずに one day (過去の)ある日, (未来の)いつか these days このごろ
- **deal** 名 取引, 扱い
- **decade** 名 10年間
- **decision** 名 ①決定, 決心 ②判決
- **definitely** 副 ①限定的に, 明確に, 確実に ②まったくそのとおり
- **depend** 動《- on [upon] ~》①~を頼る, ~をあてにする ②~による
- **describe** 動(言葉で)描写する, 特色を述べる, 説明する
- **design** 動 設計する, 企てる
- **desire** 名 欲望, 欲求, 願望
- **destiny** 名 運命, 宿命
- **destroy** 動 破壊する, 絶滅させる, 無効にする

- **detail** 名 細部,《-s》詳細
- **determination** 名 決心, 決定
- **determined** 形 決心した, 決然とした
- **different from**《be -》~と違う
- **differently** 副 (~と)異なって, 違って
- **direct** 形 まっすぐな, 直接の, 率直な, 露骨な
- **direction** 名 方向, 方角
- **disappear** 動 見えなくなる, 姿を消す, なくなる
- **divorce** 名 離婚
- **do well** 成績が良い, 成功する
- **do with** ~を処理する
- **door** 熟 next door お隣の, 隣に住む
- **doubt** 名 ①疑い, 不確かなこと ②未解決点, 困難
- **Dr. Seuss** ドクター・スース《絵本作家, 本名セオドア・スース・ガイゼル (Theodore Seuss Geisel)》
- **draw** 動 ①引く, 引っ張る ②描く
- **dream of** ~を夢見る
- **dressed** 形 服を着た

E

- **each day** 毎日, 日ごとに
- **each other** お互いに
- **each time** ~するたびに
- **earn** 動 儲ける, 稼ぐ
- **earth** 熟 on earth ①いったい ②地球上で, この世で
- **easily** 副 ①容易に, たやすく, 苦もなく ②気楽に
- **easy** 熟 take it easy 気楽にやる
- **economist** 名 経済学者
- **economy** 名 経済, 財政

Word List

- **edge** 名 ①刃 ②端, 縁
- **editor** 名 編集者, 編集長
- **educator** 名 教育者
- **effort** 名 努力(の成果)
- **either A or B** AかそれともB
- **Eleanor Roosevelt** エレノア・ルーズベルト《アメリカ合衆国第32代大統領フランクリン・ルーズベルト夫人》
- **'em** 略 themの短縮形
- **email** 名 Eメール
- **Emily** 名 エミリー《人名》
- **end** 熟 in the end とうとう, 結局, ついに
- **enough to do** ～するのに十分な
- **enthusiasm** 名 情熱, 熱意, 熱心
- **equal** 形 等しい, 均等な, 平等な
- **even if** たとえ～でも
- **even though** ～であるけれども, ～にもかかわらず
- **eventually** 副 結局は
- **every day** 毎日
- **every single day** 一日も欠かさずに
- **everybody** 代 誰でも, 皆
- **everyone** 代 誰でも, 皆
- **everything** 代 すべてのこと[もの], 何でも, 何もかも
- **evidence** 名 ①証拠, 証人 ②形跡
- **exact** 形 正確な, 厳密な, きちょうめんな
- **example** 熟 for example たとえば
- **excellent** 形 優れた, 優秀な
- **excited** 形 興奮した, わくわくした
- **excitement** 名 興奮(すること)
- **exciting** 形 興奮させる, わくわくさせる
- **exercise** 名 ①運動, 体操 ②練習 動 ①運動する, 練習する ②影響を及ぼす
- **exist** 動 存在する, 生存する, ある, いる
- **expect** 動 予期[予測]する, (当然のこととして)期待する
- **expert** 名 専門家, 熟練者, エキスパート
- **express** 動 表現する, 述べる
- **extra** 形 余分の, 臨時の
- **extraordinary** 形 異常な, 並はずれた, 驚くべき

F

- **fact** 熟 in fact つまり, 実は, 要するに
- **fail** 動 ①失敗する, 落第する[させる] ②《- to ～》～し損なう, ～できない ③失望させる
- **fair** 形 正しい, 公平[正当]な
- **fall back** 戻る
- **fall in love** 恋におちる
- **fame** 名 評判, 名声
- **famous for** 《be -》～で有名である
- **famously** 副 よく知られているように
- **fancy** 形 ①装飾的な, 見事な ②法外な, 高級な
- **far** 熟 far away 遠く離れて far from ～から遠い, ～どころか how far どのくらいの距離ですか
- **fare** 名 運賃, 料金
- **fast-moving** 形 動きの速い
- **fear** 名 ①恐れ ②心配, 不安 動 ①恐れる ②心配する
- **feed** 動 ①食物を与える ②供給する
- **feel better** 気分がよくなる
- **feel sorry for** ～をかわいそうに

思う
- **feeling** 名 感じ, 気持ち
- **female** 名 婦人, 雌
- **fence** 名 囲み, さく
- **fiction** 名 フィクション, 作り話, 小説
- **fight back** 反撃に転じる, 応戦する
- **fight over** ～のことで言い争う
- **fight with** ～と戦う
- **filmmaker** 名 映画制作者
- **find out** 見つけ出す, 気がつく, 知る, 調べる, 解明する
- **first** 熟 at first 最初は, 初めのうちは for the first time 初めて
- **first lady** 大統領夫人
- **fix** 動 修理する
- **fond** 形 ①《be - of ～》～が大好きである ②愛情の深い
- **fool** 名 ①ばか者, おろかな人 ②道化師 動 ばかにする, だます, ふざける
- **football** 名 (英国で)サッカー, (米国で)アメリカンフットボール
- **for example** たとえば
- **forgive** 動 許す, 免除する
- **forgiven** 動 forgive (許す)の過去分詞
- **fortunately** 副 幸運にも
- **forward** 副 ①前方に ②将来に向けて ③先へ, 進んで look forward to ～を期待する
- **Frank Baum** フランク・ボーム《児童文学作家, ファンタジー作家》
- **Frank Leahy** フランク・リーヒー《アメリカン・フットボール選手, コーチ》
- **Franklin D. Roosevelt** フランクリン・ルーズベルト《アメリカ合衆国第32代大統領》
- **friendship** 名 友人であること, 友情
- **front** 熟 in front of ～の前に, ～の正面に
- **full of** 《be -》～で一杯である
- **funny** 形 ①おもしろい, こっけいな ②奇妙な, うさんくさい
- **furniture** 名 家具, 備品, 調度
- **future** 熟 in the future 将来は

G

- **gain** 動 ①得る, 増す ②進歩する, 進む 名 ①増加, 進歩 ②利益, 得ること, 獲得
- **gamble** 名 賭け事, ギャンブル
- **gas** 名 ガソリン
- **general** 熟 in general 一般に, たいてい
- **generally** 副 ①一般に, だいたい ②たいてい
- **get** 熟 get ahead 進歩する, うまくいく, 出世する get along やっていく, はかどる get angry 腹を立てる get around 広まる get back 戻る, 帰る get better (病気などが)良くなる get dark 暗くなる get going 活動する get home 家に着く [帰る] get in the way 邪魔をする, 妨げになる get into trouble 面倒を起こす, 困った事になる, トラブルに巻き込まれる get offered 申し出を受ける get out ①外に出る, 出て行く, 逃げ出す ②取り出す, 抜き出す get out of ～から外へ出る [抜け出る] get out of bed 起きる, 寝床を離れる get over 乗り越える get revenge 復しゅうする get sick 病気になる, 発病する, 気分が悪くなる get there そこに到着する, 目的を達成する, 成功する get through 乗り切る, ～を通り抜ける get to (事)を始める, ～に達する [到着する] get to do ～できるようになる, ～できる機会を得る get to know 知るようになる, 知り合う get up 起き上がる, 立ち上がる

- get used to ～になじむ、～に慣れる
- get worse 悪化する
- ☐ **gift** 名 ①贈り物 ②(天賦の)才能
- ☐ **girlfriend** 名 女友だち
- ☐ **give away** ①ただで与える、贈る、譲歩する、手放す ②(素性・正体を)暴露する、馬脚を現す
- ☐ **give up** あきらめる、やめる、引き渡す
- ☐ **glitter** 名 輝き、華麗さ
- ☐ **go** 熟 get going 活動する go around 動き回る、あちらこちらに行く、回り道をする、(障害)を回避する go back to ～に帰る[戻る]、～に週る、(中断していた作業に)再び取り掛かる go by ①(時が)過ぎる、経過する ②～のそばを通る ③～に基づいて[よって]行う go for ～に出かける、～を追い求める、～を好む go home 帰宅する go into ～に入る、(仕事)に就く go out 外出する、外へ出る go over ～を越えて行く、～へ渡る go to sleep 寝る go up ①～に上がる、登る ②～に近づく、出かける ③(建物などが)建つ、立つ go with ～と一緒に行く、～と調和する、～にとても似合う go wrong 失敗する、道を踏みはずす、調子が悪くなる
- ☐ **gold** 名 金、金貨、金製品
- ☐ **golden** 形 ①金色の ②金製の ③貴重
- ☐ **good** 熟 as good as ～も同然で、ほとんど～ be good at ～が得意だ have a good time 楽しい時を過ごす
- ☐ **good-looking** 形 顔立ちのよい、ハンサムな、きれいな
- ☐ **gossip** 名 うわさ話、ゴシップ
- ☐ **governor** 名 知事
- ☐ **grand slam** 満塁ホームラン《野球》
- ☐ **grass** 名 草、牧草(地)、芝生
- ☐ **grease** 名 油脂、獣脂、グリース
- ☐ **grow into** 成長して～になる
- ☐ **grow up** 成長する、大人になる
- ☐ **guy** 名 男、やつ

H

- ☐ **habit** 名 習慣、癖、気質
- ☐ **had better** ～したほうが身のためだ、～しなさい
- ☐ **haircut** 名 散髪
- ☐ **hairstyle** 名 ヘアスタイル、髪型
- ☐ **hamburger** 名 ハンバーガー
- ☐ **hand** 熟 hand in 差し出す、提出する on the other hand 一方、他方では
- ☐ **handle** 動 取り扱う
- ☐ **happen to** たまたま～する、偶然～する
- ☐ **happening** 動 happen(起こる)の現在分詞 名 出来事、事件
- ☐ **happiness** 名 幸せ、喜び
- ☐ **hard to** 熟 ～し難い
- ☐ **Harley L. Lutz** ハーレー・L・ルッツ《経済学者、プリンストン大学教授》
- ☐ **hatch** 動 (ひなを)かえす、(ひなが)かえる
- ☐ **hate** 動 嫌う、憎む、(～するのを)いやがる
- ☐ **have a good time** 楽しい時を過ごす
- ☐ **have no idea** わからない
- ☐ **have someone over** (人)を家に呼ぶ
- ☐ **have something to say** 言いたいことがある
- ☐ **headline** 名 (新聞などの)見出し
- ☐ **heal** 動 いえる、いやす、治る、治す
- ☐ **healthy** 形 健康な、健全な、健康によい
- ☐ **hear about** ～について聞く

INSPIRATIONAL PROVERBS AND SAYINGS

- **hear from** ～から手紙[電話・返事]をもらう
- **heat** 名 熱, 暑さ
- **Herman Edwards** ハーマン・エドワーズ《アメリカン・フットボール選手, コーチ》
- **hey** 間《呼びかけ・注意を促して》おい, ちょっと ②へえ, おや, まあ
- **hidden** 動 hide（隠れる）の過去分詞
- **high-pressure job** 形 プレッシャーがきつい仕事
- **hindsight** 名 あとになっての判断, 後知恵
- **hmm** 間 ふむ, ううむ《熟考・疑問・ためらいなどを表す》
- **home** 熟 at home 在宅して, 気楽に, くつろいで get home 家に着く[帰る] go home 帰宅する
- **honest** 形 ①正直な, 誠実な, 心からの ②公正な, 感心な
- **hopefully** 副 できれば, 希望を持って
- **horrible** 形 恐ろしい, ひどい
- **horror** 名 ①恐怖, ぞっとすること ②嫌悪
- **how far** どのくらいの距離ですか
- **how to** ～する方法
- **however** 副 たとえ～でも 接 けれども, だが
- **huge** 形 巨大な, ばく大な
- **hundreds of** 何百もの～
- **hunger** 名 ①空腹, 飢え ②(～への)欲

I

- **I'm afraid (that)** 残念ながら～, 悪いけれど～
- **idea** 熟 have no idea わからない
- **if** 熟 even if たとえ～でも if only ～でありさえすれば if possible できるなら If +《主語》+ could ～できればなあ《仮定法》
- **ignore** 動 無視する, 怠る
- **imagine** 動 想像する, 心に思い描く
- **importantly** 副 重大に, もったいぶって
- **improve** 動 改善する[させる], 進歩する
- **indirectly** 副 間接(的)に, 遠回しに
- **industrialist** 名 実業家
- **ingredient** 名 成分, 原料, 材料
- **inspire** 動 ①奮い立たせる, 鼓舞する ②(感情などを)吹き込む ③霊感を与える
- **instead** 副 その代わりに instead of ～の代わりに, ～をしないで
- **interesting** 形 おもしろい, 興味を起こさせる
- **inventor** 名 発明者, 発案者
- **invest** 動 投資する, (金・精力などを)注ぐ
- **iron** 名 鉄, 鉄製のもの
- **It is ~ for someone to ...** (人)が…するのは～だ
- **itself** 代 それ自体, それ自身

J

- **Jack Welch** ジャック・ウェルチ《米ゼネラル・エレクトリック社の元会長》
- **Jim** 名 ジム《人名》
- **Jimi Hendrix** ジミ・ヘンドリックス《ミュージシャン, ギタリスト》
- **job** 熟 do a good job うまくやってのける
- **Joe** 名 ジョー《人名》
- **John** 名 ジョン《人名》

Word List

- **John F. Kennedy** ジョン・F・ケネディ《第35代アメリカ合衆国大統領》
- **Joseph P. Kennedy** ジョセフ・P・ケネディ《政治家・実業家》
- **joy** 名 喜び、楽しみ
- **judge** 動 判決をドす、裁く、判断する、評価する
- **just as** (ちょうど)であろうとおり

K

- **Kate** 名 ケイト《人名》
- **kind of** ある程度、いくらか、〜のような物[人]
- **knock** 動 ノックする、たたく、ぶつける
- **know** 熟 get to know 知るようになる、知り合う
- **knowledge** 名 知識、理解、学問

L

- **L. Frank Baum** ライマン・フランク・ボーム《児童文学作家、ファンタジー作家》
- **largely** 副 大いに、主として
- **laugh** 熟 make someone laugh (人)を笑わせる
- **laughter** 名 笑い(声)
- **lawyer** 名 弁護士、法律家
- **lead to** 〜に至る、〜に通じる、〜を引き起こす
- **learning experience** ためになる人生経験
- **least** 名 最小、最少 at least 少なくとも
- **leave 〜 alone** 〜をそっとしておく
- **leave for** 〜に向かって出発する
- **leave over** 残しておく
- **lemon** 名 レモン
- **lemonade** 名 レモネード
- **Leo Durocher** レオ・ドローチャー《プロ野球選手、監督》
- **less** 形 より小さい[少ない] 副 〜より少なく、〜ほどでなく less and less だんだん少なく〜、ますます〜でなく
- **lie** 動 ①うそをつく ②横たわる、寝る ③(ある状態に)ある、存在する 名 うそ、詐欺
- **like** 熟 like this このような、こんなふうに look like 〜のように見える、〜に似ている would like to 〜したいと思う
- **likely** 形 ①ありそうな、(〜)しそうな ②適当な 副 たぶん、おそらく
- **limit** 名 限界、《-s》範囲、境界 動 制限[限定]する
- **limited** 動 limit (制限する)の過去、過去分詞 形 限られた、限定の
- **Linda** 名 リンダ《人名》
- **line** 名 ①線、境界線 ②せりふ、一節 opening line 出だしの文句
- **lining** 名 裏地、裏当て
- **Lisa** 名 リサ《人名》
- **list** 名 名簿、目録、一覧表
- **listener** 名 聞く人、ラジオ聴取者
- **live on** 〜を糧として生きる
- **live through** (危機などを)乗り越える
- **living** 動 live (住む)の現在分詞 名 生計、生活 形 ①生きている、現存の ②使用されている ③そっくりの
- **Liza Minnelli** ライザ・ミネリ《女優、歌手》
- **load** 動 積む、詰め込む bases are loaded 満塁です
- **London** 名 ロンドン《英国の首都》
- **lonely** 形 ①孤独な、心さびしい ②ひっそりした、人里離れた
- **long** 熟 as long as 〜する以上は、

~である限りは **no longer** もはや~でない[~しない] **so long as** ~する限りは

- **look** 熟 **look for** ~を探す **look forward to** ~を期待する **look in** 中を見る、立ち寄る **look like** ~のように見える、~に似ている **look on** 傍観する、眺める **look out for** ~に気を配る、~に注意する **look over** ~越しに見る、~を見渡す **take a look at** ~をちょっと見る
- **losing** 動 負ける、失敗する、損をする
- **loss** 名 ①損失(額・物)、損害、浪費 ②失敗、敗北
- **lost to** 《be ~》~のものではない
- **love** 熟 **fall in love** 恋におちる
- **luck** 熟 **bad luck** 災難、不運、悪運

M

- **mad** 形 ①気の狂った ②逆上した、理性をなくした ③ばかげた ④(~に)熱狂[熱中]して、夢中の
- **main** 形 主な、主要な
- **make** 熟 **make a mistake** 間違いをする **make money** お金を儲ける **make noise** 音を立てる **make sense** 意味をなす、よくわかる **make someone laugh** (人)を笑わせる **make sure** 確かめる、確認する **make the most of** ~を最大限利用する **make up** 作り出す、考え出す、~を構成[形成]する **make up one's mind** 決心する
- **male** 名 男、雄
- **management** 名 ①経営、取り扱い ②運営、管理(側)
- **manager** 名 経営者、支配人、支店長、部長
- **many** 熟 **so many** 非常に多くの
- **Marilyn Monroe** マリリン・モンロー《女優》

- **mark** 動 印[記号]をつける
- **Mark Twain** マーク・トウェイン《作家、小説家》
- **married** 形 結婚した、既婚の
- **match** 名 相手、釣り合うもの
- **matter** 熟 **no matter** ~を問わず、どうでもいい **no matter how** どんなに~であろうとも
- **meaning** 名 ①意味、趣旨 ②重要性
- **means** 動 mean (意味する) の3人称単数現在 名 ①手段、方法 ②資力、財産 ③mean (中間) の複数
- **measure** 動 ①測る、(~の) 寸法がある ②評価する
- **media** 名 メディア、マスコミ、媒体
- **meeting** 動 meet (会う) の現在分詞 名 ①集まり、ミーティング、面会 ②競技会
- **memory** 名 記憶(力)、思い出
- **might** 助《mayの過去》①~かもしれない ②~してもよい、~できる
- **mind** 名 ①心、精神、考え ②知性 **make up one's mind** 決心する **state of mind** 気持ち、心理状態 動 ①気にする、いやがる ②気をつける、用心する
- **mirror** 名 鏡
- **misery** 名 ①悲惨、みじめさ ②苦痛、不幸、苦難
- **mistake** 熟 **make a mistake** 間違いをする
- **mix** 動 ①混ざる、混ぜる ②(~を)一緒にする
- **modern** 形 現代[近代]の、現代的な、最近の
- **money** 熟 **make money** お金を儲ける
- **mood** 名 気分、機嫌、雰囲気、憂うつ
- **more** 熟 **more and more** ますます **the more ~ the more …** ~すればするほどますます

WORD LIST

- **most** 熟 make the most of ~を最大限利用する
- **motivation** 名 やる気, 動機
- **move away** ①立ち去る ②移す, 動かす
- **move in** 引っ越す
- **move on** 先に進む
- **move to** ~に引っ越す
- **much** 熟 too much 過度の
- **Muhammad Ali** モハメド・アリ《元プロボクサー》
- **musician** 名 音楽家

N

- **naturally** 副 生まれつき, 自然に, 当然
- **necessary** 形 必要な, 必然の
- **negative** 形 ①否定的な, 消極的な ②負の, マイナスの, (写真が) ネガの 名 ①否定, 反対 ②ネガ, 陰画, 負数, マイナス
- **neighborhood** 名 近所(の人々), 付近
- **news** 名 報道, ニュース, 便り, 知らせ
- **newspaper** 名 新聞(紙)
- **next door** お隣の, 隣に住む
- **night** 熟 stay up all night 徹夜する
- **no longer** もはや~ない[~しない]
- **no matter** ~を問わず, どうでもいい
- **no matter how** どんなに~であろうとも
- **no one** 代 誰も[1人も]~ない
- **nobody** 代 誰も[1人も]~ない
- **noise** 名 騒音, 騒ぎ, 物音 make noise 音を立てる
- **noisy** 形 ①騒々しい, やかましい ②けばけばしい
- **none** 代 (~の)何も[誰も・少しも]…ない
- **normally** 副 普通は, 通常は
- **not** 熟 not ~ at all 少しも[全然]~ない not ~ but … ~ではなくて not always 必ずしも~であるとは限らない not at all 少しも~でない not yet まだ~してない
- **notice** 動 ①気づく, 認める ②通告する
- **now** 熟 by now 今のところ, 今ごろまでには now that 今や~だから, ~からには
- **number** 熟 a number of いくつかの~, 多くの~

O

- **object** 名 ①物, 事物 ②目的物, 対象
- **of course** もちろん, 当然
- **offer** 動 申し出る, 申し込む, 提供する 名 提案, 提供
- **offered** 熟 get offered 申し出を受ける
- **okay** 形 《許可, 同意, 満足などを表して》よろしい, 正しい 名 許可, 承認
- **once** 熟 at once すぐに, 同時に
- **one day** (過去の)ある日, (未来の)いつか
- **one of** ~の1つ[人]
- **oneself** 熟 by oneself 一人で, 自分だけで, 独力で
- **only** 熟 if only ~でありさえすれば
- **open up** 広がる, 広げる, 開く, 開ける
- **opening line** 出だしの文句
- **opportunity** 名 好機, 適当な時期[状況]

119

Inspirational Proverbs and Sayings

- **option** 名選択(の余地), 選択可能物, 選択権
- **order** 熟 in order to 〜するために, 〜しようと
- **ordinary** 形 ①普通の, 通常の ②並の, 平凡な
- **original** 形 ①始めの, 元の, 本来の ②独創的な
- **other** 熟 each other お互いに on the other hand 一方, 他方では
- **out** 熟 be out 外出している get out ①外に出る, 出て行く, 逃げ出す ②取り出す, 抜き出す get out of 〜から外へ出る[抜け出る] get out of bed 起きる, 寝床を離れる go out 外出する, 外へ出る look out for 〜に気を配る, 〜に注意する out of ①〜から外へ, 〜から抜け出して ②〜から作り出して, 〜を材料として ③〜の範囲外に, 〜から離れて ④(ある数)の中から throw out 放り出す turn out ①〜と判明する, (結局〜に)なる ②(照明などを)消す ③養成する ④出かける, 集まる ⑤外側に向く, ひっくり返す watch out 警戒[監視]する watch out for 〜に注意する work out うまくいく, 何とかなる, (問題を)解く, 考え出す, 答えが出る, 〜の結果になる
- **over** 形《be 〜》終わる
- **own** 熟 of one's own 自分自身の on one's own 自力で

P

- **paid** 動 pay (払う)の過去, 過去分詞
- **painful** 形 ①痛い, 苦しい, 痛ましい ②骨の折れる, 困難な
- **painting** 名絵(をかくこと), 絵画, 油絵
- **parent** 名 ①《-s》両親 ②先祖
- **part** 熟 take part in 〜に参加する
- **particular** 形 ①特別の ②詳細な
- **particularly** 副特に, とりわけ
- **partner** 名配偶者, 仲間, 同僚
- **passing** 動 pass (過ぎる)の現在分詞 形通り過ぎる, 一時的な
- **passion** 名情熱, (〜への)熱中, 激怒
- **past** 名過去(の出来事)
- **path** 名 ①(踏まれてできた)小道, 歩道 ②進路, 通路
- **patient** 形我慢[忍耐]強い, 根気のある 名病人, 患者
- **pattern** 名 ①柄, 型, 模様 ②手本, 模範
- **pay** 動 ①支払う, 払う, 報いる, 償う ②割に合う, ペイする pay back 返済する, お返しをする 名給料, 報い
- **penny** 名ペニー, ペンス《英国の貨幣単位。1/100ポンド》
- **personality** 名人格, 個性
- **pick up** 拾い上げる
- **picky** 形えり好みする, 小うるさい
- **place** 熟 in one place 一ヶ所に take one's place (人と)交代する, (人の)代わりをする, 後任になる
- **plan to do** 〜するつもりである
- **player** 名競技者, 選手, 演奏者, 俳優
- **pleasure** 名喜び, 楽しみ, 満足, 娯楽
- **plenty** 名十分, たくさん, 豊富
- **plenty of** たくさんの〜
- **polite** 形ていねいな, 礼儀正しい, 洗練された
- **politician** 名政治家, 政略家
- **poorly** 副へたに
- **position** 名 ①位置, 場所, 姿勢 ②地位, 身分, 職 ③立場, 状況
- **positive** 形 ①積極的な ②明確な, 明白な, 確信している ③プラスの, (写真が)ポジの 名 ①正数, プラス, 陽極 ②ポジ, 陽画

Word List

- **possible** 形 ①可能な ②ありうる, 起こりうる **if possible** できるなら
- **possibly** 副 ①あるいは, たぶん ②《否定文, 疑問文で》どうしても, できる限り, とても, なんとか
- **pour** 動 ①注ぐ, 浴びせる ②流れ出る, 流れ込む ③ざあざあ降る
- **powerful** 形 力強い, 実力のある, 影響力のある
- **preach** 動 説教する, 説く
- **prefer** 動 (～のほうを)好む, (～のほうが)よいと思う
- **prepare for** ～の準備をする
- **prepared** 形 準備[用意]のできた
- **presentation** 名 ①提出, 提示 ②実演, プレゼンテーション
- **President** 名 大統領
- **pressure** 名 押すこと, 圧力, 圧縮, 重荷
- **prevent** 動 ①妨げる, じゃまする ②予防する, 守る, 《～ from …》～が…できない[しない]ようにする
- **price** 名 値段
- **probably** 副 たぶん, あるいは
- **product** 名 ①製品, 産物 ②成果, 結果
- **progress** 名 進歩, 前進
- **promotion** 名 ①昇進 ②促進 ③宣伝販売
- **proud** 形 ①自慢の, 誇った, 自尊心のある ②高慢な, 尊大な **be proud of** ～を自慢に思う
- **proverb** 名 ことわざ, 格言
- **provide** 動 ①供給する, 用意する, (～に)備える ②規定する
- **purpose** 熟 **on purpose** わざと, 故意に
- **put down** 下に置く, ドろす
- **put in** ～の中に入れる
- **put on** ①～を身につける, 着る ②～を…の上に置く

Q

- **quickly** 副 敏速に, 急いで
- **quit** 動 やめる, 辞職する, 中止する
- **quote** 名 引用(句)

R

- **raise** 名 昇給
- **Ralph Waldo Emerson** ラルフ・ワルド・エマーソン《作家, 思想家》
- **rare** 形 まれな, 珍しい
- **ready for** 熟 《be ～》準備が整って, ～に期待する
- **realistic** 形 現実的な, 現実主義の
- **reality** 名 現実, 実在, 真実(性)
- **realize** 動 理解する, 実現する
- **relationship** 名 関係, 関連, 血縁関係
- **remind** 動 思い出させる, 気づかせる
- **reminder** 名 思い出させるもの
- **repay** 動 ①払い戻す, 返金する ②報いる, 恩返しする
- **repeat** 動 繰り返す
- **replace** 動 ①取り替える, 差し替える ②元に戻す
- **reply** 動 答える, 返事をする, 応答する
- **represent** 動 ①表現する ②意味する ③代表する
- **respect** 名 ①尊敬, 尊重 ②注意, 考慮 動 尊敬[尊重]する
- **responsibility** 名 ①責任, 義務, 義理 ②負担, 責務
- **responsible** 形 責任のある, 信頼できる, 確実な
- **result** 名 結果, 成り行き, 成績 動 (結果として)起こる, 生じる, 結局～になる
- **resume** 動 再び始める, 再開する

Inspirational Proverbs and Sayings

- **return** 熟 in return お返しとして
- **revenge** 名 復しゅう get revenge 復しゅうする
- **risk** 名 危険
- **risky** 形 危険な, 冒険的な, リスクの伴う
- **rocket** 名 ロケット
- **role** 名 ①(劇などの)役 ②役割, 任務
- **Roman** 名 ローマ人[市民]
- **romance** 名 恋愛(関係・感情), 恋愛[空想・冒険]小説
- **romantic** 形 ロマンチックな, 空想的な
- **Rome** 名 ①ローマ《イタリアの首都》②古代ローマ(帝国)
- **ruin** 動 破滅させる
- **run into** ~に駆け込む, ~の中に走って入る

S

- **same** 熟 the same ~ as [that] ……と同じ(ような)~
- **sauce** 名 ソース
- **say** 熟 have something to say 言いたいことがある
- **saying** 動 say (言う)の現在分詞 名 ことわざ, 格言, 発言
- **scared** 形 おびえた, びっくりした
- **scary** 形 恐ろしい, こわい, 臆病な
- **score** 名 (競技の)得点, スコア
- **secret** 名 秘密, 神秘
- **see ~ as ...** ~を…と考える
- **seem** 動 (~に)見える, (~のように)思われる
- **seem to be** ~であるように思われる
- **senior management position** 上級管理職

- **sense** 名 ①感覚, 感じ ②《-s》意識, 正気, 本性 ③常識, 分別, センス ④意味 make sense 意味をなす, よくわかる sense of control コントロール感
- **sentence** 名 文
- **separate** 形 分かれた, 別れた, 別々の
- **serious** 形 ①まじめな, 真剣な ②重大な, 深刻な, (病気などが)重い
- **seriously** 副 ①真剣に, まじめに ②重大に
- **shared** 形 共用の, 共有の
- **shark** 名 サメ, 他人を食いものにする人
- **shine** 動 ①光る, 輝く ②光らせる, 磨く
- **should have done** ~すべきった(のにしなかった)
- **show up** 顔を出す, 現れる
- **shy** 形 内気な, 恥ずかしがりの, 臆病な
- **sick** 熟 get sick 病気になる, 発病する, 気分が悪くなる
- **side** 名 側, 横, そば, 斜面 side by side 並んで
- **silver** 名 銀, 銀貨, 銀色 形 銀製の
- **silver lining** 希望の兆し
- **similar** 形 同じような, 類似した, 相似の
- **simply** 副 ①簡単に ②単に, ただ ③まったく, 完全に
- **singer** 名 歌手, シンガー
- **single** 形 ①たった1つの ②1人用の, それぞれの ③独身の ④片道の every single day 一日も欠かさずに
- **situation** 名 ①場所, 位置 ②状況, 境遇, 立場
- **skill** 名 ①技能, 技術 ②上手, 熟練
- **slam** 熟 grand slam 満塁ホームラン《野球》
- **sleep** 熟 go to sleep 寝る

122

WORD LIST

- **slice** 名薄切りの1枚, 部分
- **smart** 形①利口な, 抜け目のない ②きちんとした, 洗練された ③激しい, ずきずきする
- **smoke** 動喫煙する, 煙を出す 名煙, 煙状のもの
- **so** 熟 and so on ～など, その他もろもろ or so ～かそこらで so ～ as to …するほど～で so ～ that … 非常に～なので so long as ～する限りは so many 非常に多くの so that ～するために, それで, ～できるように
- **society** 名社会, 世間
- **some time** いつか, そのうち
- **somebody** 代誰か, ある人
- **someday** 副いつか, そのうち
- **someone** 代ある人, 誰か
- **something** 代①ある物, 何か ②いくぶん, 多少 something to do 何か～すべきこと
- **sometimes** 副時々, 時たま
- **somewhere** 副①どこかへ[に] ②いつか, およそ
- **sorry** 熟 feel sorry for ～をかわいそうに思う
- **sound like** ～のように聞こえる
- **sour** 形①すっぱい ②不機嫌な
- **speak up** 率直に話す, はっきりしゃべる
- **spoil** 動①台なしにする, だめになる, だめになる ②甘やかす
- **squeaky** 形キーキーいう, きしる
- **state** 名①あり様, 状態 ②国家,(アメリカなどの)州 ③階層, 地位 state of mind 気持ち, 心理状態
- **stay up all night** 徹夜する
- **steady** 形①しっかりした, 安定した, 落ち着いた ②堅実な, まじめな
- **steak** 名ステーキ
- **Stephen King** スティーヴン・キング《小説家》
- **stolen** 動 steal (盗む)の過去分詞
- **stone** 名石, 小石
- **strength** 名①力, 体力 ②長所, 強み ③強度, 濃度
- **stress** 名①圧力 ②ストレス ③強勢
- **stressful** 形ストレスの多い
- **strike** 動打つ, ぶつかる
- **strongly** 副強く, 頑丈に, 猛烈に, 熱心に
- **stubborn** 形頑固な, 強情な
- **stuff** 名もの, 持ち物, 事柄
- **substitute** 名代用品, 代理人
- **succeed** 動①成功する ②(～の)跡を継ぐ
- **success** 名成功, 幸運, 上首尾
- **successful** 形成功した, うまくいった
- **such ~ as ...** …のような～
- **such a** そのような
- **such as** たとえば～, ～のような
- **suit** 名スーツ, 背広
- **sunrise** 名日の出
- **supply** 名供給(品), 給与, 補充
- **support** 動①支える, 支持する ②養う, 援助する 名①支え, 支持 ②援助, 扶養
- **supposed** 形想定された be supposed to ～することになっている, ～するはずである
- **sure** 熟 for sure 確かに make sure 確かめる, 確認する
- **surely** 副確かに, きっと
- **surface** 名①表面, 水面 ②うわべ, 外見 on the surface 外面は, うわべは
- **surprised** 動 surprise (驚かす)の過去, 過去分詞 形驚いた
- **surprising** 動 surprise (驚かす)の現在分詞 形驚くべき, 意外な
- **survive** 動①生き残る, 存続する,

なんとかなる ②長生きする, 切り抜ける
- **sweat** 名 汗 動 汗をかく

T

- **take** 熟 take a look at ～をちょっと見る take a walk 散歩をする take away ①連れ去る ②取り上げる, 奪い去る ③取り除く take control of ～を制御[管理]する, 支配する take it easy 気楽にやる take off (衣服を)脱ぐ, 取り去る, ～を取り除く, 離陸する, 出発する take one's place (人と)交代する, (人)の代わりをする, 後任になる take part in ～に参加する
- **talent** 名 才能, 才能ある人
- **talented** 形 才能のある, 有能な
- **tango** 名 タンゴ《ダンス》
- **task** 名 (やるべき)仕事, 職務, 課題 動 仕事を課す, 負担をかける
- **taste** 名 ①味, 風味 ②好み, 趣味 動 味がする, 味わう
- **taxi** 名 タクシー 動 ①(飛行機が滑走路を)移動する ②タクシーで行く
- **technology** 名 テクノロジー, 科学技術
- **television** 名 テレビ
- **terribly** 副 ひどく
- **thanks to** ～のおかげで, ～の結果
- **that** 熟 now that 今や～だから, ～からには
- **That's too bad.** 残念だ.
- **there** 熟 get there そこに到達する, 目的を達成する, 成功する over there あそこに there is no way ～する見込みはない
- **these days** このごろ
- **thick** 形 厚い, 密集した, 濃厚な 副 厚く, 濃く 名 最も厚い[強い・濃い]部分

- **think of** ～のことを考える, ～を思いつく, 考え出す
- **this** 熟 like this このような, こんなふうに
- **Thomas Edison** トーマス・エジソン《発明家》
- **though** 接 ①～にもかかわらず, ～だが ②たとえ～でも even though ～であるけれども, ～にもかかわらず 副 しかし
- **throw out** 放り出す
- **'til** 接 = till
- **till** 前 ～まで(ずっと) 接 ～(する)まで
- **time** 熟 any time いつでも at the time そのころ, 当時は each time ～するたびに for the first time 初めて have a good time 楽しい時を過ごす next time 次回に on time 時間どおりに some time いつか, そのうち
- **timing** 名 タイミング
- **tired** 動 tire (疲れる)の過去, 過去分詞 形 ①疲れた, くたびれた ②あきた, うんざりした be tired of ～に飽きて[うんざりして]いる
- **tough** 形 堅い, 丈夫な, たくましい, 骨の折れる, 困難な
- **trash** 名 ①くず, ごみ ②くだらないもの[人]
- **traveling** 名 旅行
- **treasure** 名 財宝, 貴重品, 宝物 動 秘蔵する
- **treat** 動 ①扱う ②治療する ③おごる 名 ①おごり, もてなし, ごちそう ②楽しみ
- **trouble** 熟 get into trouble 面倒を起こす, 困った事になる, トラブルに巻き込まれる in trouble 面倒な状況で, 困って
- **true** 熟 come true 実現する
- **truly** 副 本当に, 真に
- **trust** 動 信用[信頼]する, 委託する

Word List

- 名信用, 信頼, 委託
- **truth** 名 ①真理, 事実, 本当 ②誠実, 忠実さ
- **turn away** 向こうへ行く, 追い払う, (顔を)そむける, 横を向く
- **turn into** ~に変わる
- **turn off** ①興味を失う, ~にうんざりする ②~を止める, (照明などを)消す ③(道から)それる, (道が)~から分かれる
- **turn on** ①~の方を向く ②(スイッチなどを)ひねってつける, 出す
- **turn out** ①~と判明する, (結局~に)なる ②(照明などを)消す ③養成する ④出かける, 集まる ⑤外側に向く, ひっくり返す
- **two-way street** 名 2車線道路, 相互的なもの, 相互的な関係

U

- **ugly** 形 ①醜い, ぶかっこうな ②いやな, 不快な, 険悪な
- **uh** 間 あー, あのー, ええと
- **uncommon** 形 珍しい, まれな
- **understanding** 動 understand (理解する)の現在分詞 名 理解, 意見の一致, 了解 形 理解のある, 思いやりのある
- **undo** 動 ①ほどく, はずす ②元に戻す, 取り消す
- **unfortunately** 副 不幸にも, 運悪く
- **unhappy** 形 不運な, 不幸な
- **United States** 名 アメリカ合衆国《国名》
- **universe** 名 《the - /the U-》宇宙, 全世界
- **unkind** 形 不親切な, 意地の悪い
- **unless** 接 もし~でなければ, ~しなければ
- **unusual** 形 普通でない, 珍しい, 見[聞き]慣れない
- **unwilling** 形 気が進まない, 不本意の
- **up** 熟 be up to ~の責任[義務]である up to ~まで, ~に至るまで, ~に匹敵して
- **used** 動《-to》よく~したものだ, 以前は~であった 形 ①慣れている, 《get [become] - to》~に慣れてくる ②使われた, 中古の
- **useless** 形 役に立たない, 無益な

V

- **valuable** 形 貴重な, 価値のある, 役に立つ
- **value** 名 価値, 値打ち, 価格 動 評価する, 値をつける, 大切にする
- **vegetable** 名 野菜, 青物 形 野菜の, 植物(性)の
- **vision** 名 ①視力 ②先見, 洞察力

W

- **wait for** ~を待つ
- **wake up** 起きる, 目を覚ます
- **walk** 熟 take a walk 散歩をする
- **wallet** 名 札入れ
- **Walt Disney** ウォルト・ディズニー《映画制作者, 実業家》
- **warning** 動 warn (警告する)の現在分詞 名 警告, 警報
- **watch out** 警戒[監視]する
- **watch out for** ~に注意する
- **way** 熟 along the way 途中で, これまでに, この先 get in the way 邪魔をする, 妨げになる there is no way ~する見込みはない way of ~する方法 way to ~する方法
- **weatherman** 名 天気予報士

INSPIRATIONAL PROVERBS AND SAYINGS

- **well** 熟 do well 成績が良い、成功する
- **western** 形①西の、西側の ②《W-》西洋の 名《W-》西部劇、ウェスタン
- **what ... for** 熟 どんな目的で
- **What about ~?** 熟 ~についてあなたはどう思いますか。~はどうですか。
- **whatever** 代①《関係代名詞》~するものは何でも ②どんなこと[もの]が~とも 形①どんな~でも ②《否定文・疑問文で》少しの~も、何らかの
- **wheel** 名①輪、車輪、《the-》ハンドル ②旋回 動①回転する[させる] ②~を押す
- **whether** 接 ~かどうか、~かまたは…、~であろうとなかろうと whether or not ~かどうか
- **whole** 形全体の、すべての、完全な、満~、丸~ 名《the-》全体、全部
- **whom** 代①誰を[に] ②《関係代名詞》~するところの人、そしてその人を
- **Why not?** どうしてだめなのですか。いいですとも。ぜひそうしよう!
- **will have done** ~してしまっているだろう《未来進行形》
- **Will you ~?** ~してくれませんか。
- **winner** 名勝利者、成功者
- **winning** 動 win(勝つ)の現在分詞 名勝つこと、勝利、《-s》賞金 形勝った、優勝の
- **wisdom** 名知恵、賢明(さ)
- **wish for** 所望する
- **Wizard of Oz**『オズの魔法使い』《児童文学》
- **Woody Allen** ウディ・アレン《映画監督、俳優》
- **work** 熟 at work 働いて、仕事中で、(機械が)稼動中で work in ~の分野で働く、~に入り込む work of ~の仕事 work on ~で働く、~に取り組む、~を説得する、~に効く work out うまくいく、何とかなる、(問題を)解く、考え出す、答えが出る、~の結果になる
- **world** 熟 in the world 世界で world of 大量の、無数の
- **world-famous** 形世界的に有名な
- **worm** 名虫、虫けらのような人
- **worried** 動 worry(悩む)の過去、過去分詞 形心配そうな、不安げな
- **worried about** 《be-》(~のことで)心配している、~が気になる[かかる]
- **worry about** 熟 ~のことを心配する
- **worse** 形いっそう悪い、より劣った、よりひどい get worse 悪化する 副いっそう悪く
- **worst** 形《the-》最も悪い、いちばんひどい 副最も悪く、いちばんひどく 名《the-》最悪の事態[人・物]
- **worth** 形(~の)価値がある、(~)しがいがある 名価値、値打ち
- **would like to** ~したいと思う
- **Would you ~?** ~してくださいませんか。
- **wound** 名傷 動①負傷させる、(感情を)害する ②wind(巻く)の過去、過去分詞
- **wow** 間《驚き、喜び、苦痛などを表して》うわあ!、ああ!
- **writer** 名書き手、作家
- **wrong** 熟 go wrong 失敗する、道を踏みはずす、調子が悪くなる

Y

- **yeah** 間 うん、そうだね
- **yet** 熟 not yet まだ~してない
- **Yogi Berra** ヨギ・ベラ《プロ野球選手、監督》

E-CAT

English **C**onversational **A**bility **T**est
国際英語会話能力検定

● E-CATとは…
英語が話せるようになるためのテストです。インターネットベースで、30分であなたの発話力をチェックします。

www.ecatexam.com

iTEP

● iTEP®とは…
世界各国の企業、政府機関、アメリカの大学300校以上が、英語能力判定テストとして採用。オンラインによる90分のテストで文法、リーディング、リスニング、ライティング、スピーキングの5技能をスコア化。iTEP®は、留学、就職、海外赴任などに必要な、世界に通用する英語力を総合的に評価する画期的なテストです。

www.itepexamjapan.com

ラダーシリーズ

Inspirational Proverbs and Sayings
心に響く英語のことわざ・名言100

2011年8月22日　第1刷発行
2025年7月6日　第11刷発行

著　者　レベッカ・ミルナー

発行者　賀川　洋

発行所　IBCパブリッシング株式会社
　　　　〒162-0804 東京都新宿区中里町29番3号
　　　　菱秀神楽坂ビル
　　　　Tel. 03-3513-4511　Fax. 03-3513-4512
　　　　www.ibcpub.co.jp

© IBC Publishing, Inc. 2011

印刷　株式会社シナノパブリッシングプレス
装丁　伊藤 理恵
組版データ　Sabon Roman+Frutiger 55 Roman

落丁本・乱丁本は、小社宛にお送りください。送料小社負担にてお取り替えいたします。
本書の無断複写（コピー）は著作権法上での例外を除き禁じられています。

Printed in Japan
ISBN 978-4-7946-0096-7